# Success Favors
# Well-Prepared Teachers

# Success Favors Well-Prepared Teachers

## Developing Routines and Relationships to Improve School Culture

Todd Scott Parker, Candice Dowd Barnes, and Patricia Kohler-Evans

ROWMAN & LITTLEFIELD
*Lanham • Boulder • New York • London*

Published by Rowman & Littlefield
A wholly owned subsidiary of The Rowman & Littlefield Publishing Group, Inc.
4501 Forbes Boulevard, Suite 200, Lanham, Maryland 20706
www.rowman.com

Unit A, Whitacre Mews, 26-34 Stannary Street, London SE11 4AB

Copyright © 2016 by Todd Scott Parker, Candice Dowd Barnes, and Patricia Kohler-Evans

*All rights reserved.* No part of this book may be reproduced in any form or by any electronic or mechanical means, including information storage and retrieval systems, without written permission from the publisher, except by a reviewer who may quote passages in a review.

British Library Cataloguing in Publication Information Available

**Library of Congress Cataloging-in-Publication Data Available**
ISBN: 978-1-4758-2702-6 (cloth : alk. paper)
ISBN: 978-1-4758-2703-3 (pbk. : alk. paper)
ISBN: 978-1-4758-2704-0 (electronic)

∞™ The paper used in this publication meets the minimum requirements of American National Standard for Information Sciences—Permanence of Paper for Printed Library Materials, ANSI/NISO Z39.48-1992.

Printed in the United States of America

# Contents

| | |
|---|---|
| Foreword | vii |
| Preface | ix |
| Acknowledgments | xi |

**SECTION I: WHY ARE GENUINE RELATIONSHIPS AND ROUTINES SO IMPORTANT?**     **1**

| | | |
|---|---|---|
| 1 | Creating a Context | 3 |
| 2 | The Importance of Developing Relationships and Routines | 9 |
| 3 | The Interaction Congruence Theory | 19 |
| 4 | Meet Alexander Crummell Academy | 25 |

**SECTION II: INTEGRATING RELATIONSHIPS AND ROUTINES: THE RELATIONSHIP MANAGEMENT SYSTEM (RMS)™**     **35**

| | | |
|---|---|---|
| 5 | Monitor 2 Modify (M2M) | 37 |
| 6 | Relationship Management Pathways (RMP) | 51 |
| 7 | D.E.P.T.H. Anchor Strategy | 67 |
| 8 | P.R.P.L.E. Sandwich Strategy | 83 |

## SECTION III: REFLECTION AND APPLICATION 93

9   Alexander Crummell Academy—Present Day       95
10  Final Thoughts and Next Steps                105

About the Authors                                109

# Foreword

*Success Favors Well-Prepared Teachers* is a book about building relationships among students, teaching teams, administrators, family members, and a variety of other colleagues. But it is more than that; it is a toolbox of practical strategies that can be used to help people groups set goals, identify ideals, and dream. Of the many authors who have written books about the management of classrooms, none approach the topic as the present authors do.

There are thousands of good books on classroom management that cover the predictable topics, including the first six weeks of school, setting limits, classroom routines and procedures, family support, guidance versus management, and positive discipline. This book, however, is unique in that it very effectively adds an insightful perspective on developing routines and relationships.

The strategies offered throughout the book are very practical and can be easily employed without mental overload, intervention substitutions, and lengthy professional development impositions. Rather than widespread school-wide modifications, the authors' strategies involve a change in attitude and perspective. Most important, the book is easily readable and written with passion, creativity, and enough examples that can be implemented among the reading audience. In short, it is a very "reader-friendly" book.

In my forty-five years in the field of classroom management, I have yet to encounter a book that is so effective in describing the importance of building relationships in such a strategic and calculated way. Since the publishing of *A Nation at Risk*, the passage of the No Child Left Behind Act in 2001, and the more recent emphasis on Common Core Standards, there has been information overload on strategies for achieving successful outcomes for students. However, most of the strategies overlook or minimize some very significant nonacademic dimensions of schooling such as building relationships. This book underscores the fact that understanding and addressing factors beyond traditional classroom management strategies is not only important—it is imperative.

Learning is more than an academic exercise. It is also an emotional and affective life experience. The authors understand this perfectly and have organized the book to address strategies for aligning routines and relationships with instruction and interactions in a provocative, engaging, and visionary manner. Anyone who reads *Success Favors Well-Prepared Teachers* will be impacted by its message and will view relationship building in a totally different way.

Mark J. Cooper, PhD, LPC<br>
University of Central Arkansas<br>
Professor in the Department of Elementary, Literacy,<br>
and Special Education<br>
Director of the Mashburn Center for Learning

# Preface

Imagine a classroom where the teacher sits at his/her desk and tells students what they should learn without ever attempting to make the learning real and authentic for them. The teacher doesn't bother to find out who the students are, who they would like to become, what they are interested in, what their family life is like, what areas they are struggling in, or where they experience success.

Rarely does the teacher engage students in discussions, reflections, or critical thinking. Students complete worksheet after worksheet, never really making any real connections to the content or to the teacher. Every day the routines and expectations change. Students have little sense of academic safety—feeling confident to take risks and to share their knowledge. It is truly a classroom that lacks academic courage or integrity.

Now, imagine a classroom where the teacher is invested in learning who students are and who they would like to become. In this classroom, the teacher finds ways to connect student learning to authentic and real experiences. Perhaps the teacher goes so far as to create a classroom environment where students know what to expect—an environment where there are clear routines, expectations, and norms. He/she is relentless in making sure that every student has an opportunity to demonstrate learning that connects with their learning style. Furthermore, the teacher makes sure to model perseverance and provides examples and opportunities for students to develop other social and emotional competencies.

In this classroom the students are engaged in small and whole group instruction. They ask questions and are encouraged to think deeply about the content, and how the content affects their lives and the lives of others. They feel confident in taking academic risks and are highly motivated to learn. The teacher enters the classroom everyday determined to make sure that his/her students are successful.

If you were a student, which classroom would you like to be a part of? If you were a parent, whose classroom would you want your child to be enrolled in? If you were an administrator, which classroom and teacher would you support and be most proud of? Which of the two classrooms might foster better results—results that translate into higher academic performance, increased social and emotional learning, and positive interactions? Which of the two classrooms promote an environment that supports respect and positive interactions?

Relationships and routines matter. They matter in your home, in your office, in your place of worship, in a school, and certainly, in the classroom. Few people will readily admit that they have poor interpersonal skills. Fewer people will admit to having less than effective routines, expectations, and systems to promote a results-oriented climate in their classroom, school, and/or work environment. Yet, many novice and veteran teachers report relationships, respect, and behavioral issues as their greatest challenges!

Think about this. Have you ever had a boss—a supervisor—who had a difficult time connecting with you? Maybe this person was rude, arrogant, a micromanager, or maybe they were self-absorbed and failed to see your humanity. Maybe you have experienced numerous dreadful family holiday gatherings where, if there was just a bit more structure and some basic routines, things might have seemed less chaotic and stressful.

On the other hand, perhaps you've sat in a seminar, workshop or classroom where you knew what to expect, you knew what was coming next, you had a clear understanding of the requirements and you knew your role as the learner-participant. Have you ever had an opportunity to be nurtured and coached by a great mentor, teacher, and leader who cultivated a sense of purpose, success, and achievement in your life and career? While this topic of relationship and routines can be generalized broadly to apply to other professions, the authors will focus on how relationships and routines can improve school culture and climate.

More specifically, the authors will present a system of strategies—the Relationship Management System (RMS)™. Each strategy in this system is based on the authors' Interaction Congruence Theory (ICT), which will be explained in more detail in chapter 3. This theory is comprised of various components of relatedness that support student achievement, positive interactions, and social and emotional learning.

# Acknowledgments

The authors would like to dedicate this book to educators, who are truly preparing and have prepared themselves to make a difference in the lives of children. Thank you for helping the next generation of young people find their paths toward success.

The authors would also like to thank Lauren V. Hall for creating the Relation Management System (RMS) graphics seen throughout the book. Todd would like to specifically thank Lonnie Hunter, Shalonda Randle, and Dot Jeter for being instrumental in encouraging him to perfect and implement the strategies presented in the book.

To all of our families and friends who have empowered and motivated us, who have been our voices of reason and our greatest supporters, thank you! This book, which we hope will find a place in the hearts and minds of exceptional educators, could not have been written without your encouragement. We are grateful for your presence, and for your continued love and guidance in our lives.

*Section I*

# WHY ARE GENUINE RELATIONSHIPS AND ROUTINES SO IMPORTANT?

Developing relationships and routines with students is equally as important as developing lesson plans. Likewise, creating a classroom environment where students understand the routines, expectations, feel safe to take risks, make mistakes, and can demonstrate their process of thinking is critical.

Research suggests that when teachers develop genuine relationships with students, parents, and colleagues, students' academic performance, as well as their social and emotional development, increases (Jones, Bailey & Jacob, 2014; 2009; Witmer, 2005; Morganett, 2001; Shiller, 2005; Rogers & Renard, 1999). When students are engaged by a teacher with whom they make a connection, they are more likely to engage in their work. They are more likely to make the learning meaningful. They are more likely to perform at a higher level, take risks, and develop interpersonal skills needed for learning and life.

When opening a dialogue on understanding how relationships and routines drive success, it is important to start with a few reflection questions—questions designed to help you honestly contemplate your abilities, skills, and personality traits that can make relationships both challenging and successful. These questions will also, perhaps, lend credence to the need for establishing, strengthening, or enhancing your routines for life and learning.

### REFLECT. THINK. CONNECT.

Think about the following questions, and reflect on how you might make connection to the information and your practices in the classroom and beyond.

- How do your relationships and interactions with students, colleagues, coworkers, parents, and other professionals yield positive, effective, and performance-driven results?
- In what ways are you confident that your routines, expectations, classroom, and school systems produce positive results for students and teachers? What is the evidence that affirms or confirms your confidence?

Much of the information presented in this book will address the relationships and routines in the classrooms with students. However, the authors will provide several applications and inferences to how this information applies to the relationships with others in our school buildings, including school leaders, counselors, support personnel, parents and other professionals. The bottom line is this: the relationships you develop, and/or strengthen, along with the routines set in classrooms, will greatly impact student success.

*Chapter 1*

# Creating a Context

In a groundbreaking study conducted in 1971, researchers intended to measure the impact of work-study programs on low-income young adult males in middle and high school. Ahlstrom and Havighurst (1971) found that these young boys, and especially the young men of color, were indeed faced with many challenging obstacles—obstacles that deferred their American dream, altered their paths, or in some cases, decimated their futures.

However, they also found that for the young people who overcame their neighborhood, family, academic and social challenges, it was the adult teachers and mentors, particularly the male teachers, who developed authentic relationships with them and changed their life's trajectory. It was the adults who provided a sense of stability and set routines that positively impacted their students' lives. It was through the interactions and the relationships the adults formed with these young men that their futures were most impacted.

Other researchers have asserted the same or similar findings. Classrooms and schools where students feel cared for, where there are opportunities to develop quality relationships, where individuals feel listened to, where practices and principles translate into routines are highly successful (Jones et al., 2014; Rogers & Renard, 1999). In these environments, students and teachers strive for excellence and work to build their social capital to support success in the classroom, throughout the school, and in many cases, in the community (Jones et al., 2014; Hargreaves & Fullan, 2013; Shiller, 2008; Witmer, 2005).

## CURRENT PERSPECTIVES ON RELATIONSHIPS AND ROUTINES

Fast-forward through the No Child Left Behind era, and various other educational policies all aimed at teaching children to read, write, solve intricate mathematical equations, and such. What is missing from these policies and initiatives? One area that has not been fully addressed over the past decades of policies designed to teach children traditional academic content is the idea that the character and social and emotional development of the teacher should also be considered.

As a teacher, it is important that you identify the characteristics that make you skilled at creating a culture of success in the classroom, where students can take all they have learned with them throughout life. However, relationships and routines reach beyond the classroom and can affect the overall school culture. Therefore, school leaders, administrators, counselors, parents, and other school professionals are also accountable for creating a positive school culture. These traits, dispositions, and characteristics should also be examined.

The truth is, a love for children does not always equate to a love of teaching, and not everyone who is a teacher possesses the dispositions and characteristics to be an effective and high-quality teacher. Moreover, children do not do as we say, just because we said it. Creating a classroom environment where routines and procedures are respected requires one to be consistent and repetitious. It can be challenging, but is necessary to support a culture of learning and to engage children in developing their and emotional skills. All of which can enhance their success both in and out of the classroom.

When considering how results are evidenced school-wide, there are other relationships and routines that must also be considered. For example, school leaders need to be skilled at developing, managing, and coaching relationships and routines. Counselors need to involve themselves in working with all students to support success and achievement. Support staff must engage students and colleagues in relationship-building opportunities and support the routines of the school as well. Parents must also understand and respect policies and routines and cultivate relationships with school staff.

The authors of this book concur with Ahlstrom and Havighurst (1971), and others, that the person doing the teaching is as important, if not more, than the content being taught. The tone and characteristics of the environment, including the routines established, can make a difference in achievement and performance. In essence, content is best learned when students have an adult who sets routines, builds quality and effective relationships, and provides authentic meaning for the learning, where results will be evidenced through growth, proficiency, and mastery. Schools function successfully when the leaders understand the importance of developing quality relationships with student, staff, and parents and all parties work together to achieve results.

It is therefore suggested that developing relationships and routines with students can greatly support their overall success and learning. When one develops a relationship with a student, it can activate the student's social and emotional learning, as well as their cognition. Therefore, students are more likely to be motivated to learn when they feel good about learning. Certainly, when the teacher makes a deliberate effort to positively connect and engage with students, those students will engage more deeply in the content, feel more capable, and are more willing to take risks.

## GLOSSARY OF TERMS

In the writing of this book, the authors will be introducing the reader to several ideas that they have developed as a result of their experiences in working with students of all ages. The reader is encouraged to employ the various ideas in his/her practice. In an effort to ensure understanding, the authors have defined specific terms that will be referred to throughout the book. These terms will help the reader incorporate the suggested practices in an efficient and effective manner. The terms are defined below.

**Relationship**—the way in which two or more people are connected to each other and the interactions that occur between those people.
**Relationship Pathway**—a route, or a specified way in which people seek attention, and are connected to or interact with others.
**Technique**—a task, or an efficient way of doing something.
**Routine**—a regularly followed sequence of actions or techniques.
**Strategy**—plan of action, by design, to achieve an overall goal.
**Interaction Deprived**—a lack of reciprocal benefit of human relatedness.
**Interaction Deprived Student**—a young person who is lacking the benefit of a reciprocal, genuine relationship.

## HOW WILL THIS BOOK IMPROVE MY SKILLS?

Covey (1989) suggests that one should make an effort to understand before trying to be understood. Rogers and Renard (1999) believe that understanding someone else is one of the two primary principles that set the foundation for a six standard framework designed to promote "relationship-driven teaching" (p. 34). Therefore, in order to truly obtain the desired results, one must focus on developing and strengthening quality relationships and developing effective, consistent routines for all students. By doing so, you will remain focused and invested in the humanity that is represented in your classroom. You will create a bridge to make their learning, academic and social and emotional, real and genuine. Most importantly, you will:

- Create patterns of positive interactions.
- Establish a climate of trust and support.
- Cultivate an environment where learning expectations are high.
- Decrease student misbehavior by increasing student engagement.
- Maintain students' dignity and foster their academic integrity.
- Establish a tone of respect, rapport, and relatedness.
- Develop effective routines and classroom procedures.
- Understand how the students' motivations, desires, and histories may impact their learning and behavior.

This book will integrate two concepts—relationships and routines. Together these concepts work to support a positive school culture, climate, and classroom environment. Teachers will be provided with strategies to enhance the expectations and procedures designed to manage student behaviors. In addition, social and emotional learning opportunities for students will be supported. The authors will introduce a system of relationships techniques, strategies, routines, a communication and feedback method, and other approaches, all of which can be used in the classroom and throughout life. All of this will support a culture of learning enhanced by relatedness and positive interactions.

This book is written to guide the reader through various examples, scenarios, and reflections that showcase how each strategy is used in context. Chapter 2 is a review of current literature that is foundational to the importance and purpose of developing and maintaining quality relationships and interactions, and developing routines. Chapter 3 introduces the Interaction Congruence Theory (ICT) which explains how various approaches of relatedness (i.e., personality, relationship, rapport, respect, responsiveness, and routines), work in concert to support positive interactions, student engagement, and performance.

Chapter 4 introduces a fictional school, the Alexander Crummell Academy. While Crummell is fictional, it is representative of situations and scenarios that you might find in schools throughout the country. Essential staff will be presented, and those characters will be highlighted in section II—chapters 5 through 8.

Section II is the heart of the book. Each chapter presents a component of the Relationship Management System (RMS)™. RMS™ was developed by Todd Scott Parker and implemented in various school settings. Chapter 5 presents Monitor 2 Modify—a three-pronged strategy used to differentiate behavioral expectations. Chapter 6 introduces a specified way to identify the common Relationship Management Pathways (RMPs) represented in classrooms. Chapter 7 highlights the D.E.P.T.H. Anchor Strategy—a strategy to use when a more intense behavioral invention is needed to resolve potentially volatile situations. The final chapter in section II, chapter 8, is the P.R.P.L.E. Sandwich Strategy. This acronym represents a communication strategy comprised of several techniques that can be used with students, parents, colleagues, and others to engage in meaningful conversations.

The final section of this book is comprised of two chapters. Chapter 9 will continue the journey of the Crummell Academy into next school year. The reader will be presented with more scenarios to reflect upon. Chapter 10 will conclude the book. The reader will review the strategies presented in the book, further steps for implementing the strategies effectively, and where to find more information on workshops and professional development opportunities related to the strategies.

## FINAL THOUGHTS

It is essential that you reflect a strong character and a solid constitution, meaning that you are willing and determined to provide a safe, emotionally secure environment for learning to flourish—academically, as well as socially and emotionally. It means that you understand how your traits, dispositions, and characteristics can hinder or help the culture and climate. This effort to display a strong character and constitution-firmness will promote the genuineness of your own humanity. It allows others, especially your students, to see you as real, authentic, and even, normal. It also allows you as the teacher to create connections with your students that oftentimes will be as impactful to their lives as the academic content you teach.

You have the power to motivate and positively impact your students' lives, learning, and futures. Acknowledge the desire of students to have a classroom environment that invites them to learn, to grow stronger, and to develop their social-emotional skills. Trust that your students want to perform at a high level of academic proficiency. They need you to believe in them despite their backgrounds, histories, or even your biases. Create a space and place for them to take academic risks, to exercise self-control and responsibility for their behaviors and actions.

It is well understood that the change can be gradual. Therefore, creating relationships and routines may not always have an instantaneous effect on a student's behavior or the classroom environment. It will take some time to build and strengthen students' knowledge and skills of the classroom management routines and relationship strategies, just as it takes time for students to learn academic content.

However, with consistent implementation and utilization of the strategies presented in this book, the impact can be substantial. Students will gain confidence in your resolve to ensure that the classroom is a safe place for learning.

They will grow to understand that you are preparing them for success by your making an investment in their learning, lives, and futures.

Additionally, there is the potential for the impact of the relationships you create with your students and others to be long-lasting. It might even positively affect their behavior, attitudes, temperament, and self-awareness, both in and out of the classroom. As the title indicates, well-prepared teachers foster success—success for themselves and success for their students.

Make relationships and routines count. Students and others should walk into your classroom with the understanding that you have an authentic and effective management system—a system that responds to the needs of all classroom citizens. While everyone in the classroom community is responsible for what occurs within it, the teacher is responsible for leading, guiding, and facilitating the classroom culture and climate. This type of strong and resilient classroom is greatly enhanced by the genuine relationships and routines that guide expectations.

In the next chapter, relationships and routines will be more deeply explored through a review of the literature on these two concepts. In subsequent chapters, the powerful link between routines and relationships will be examined. In many ways, these constructs are interdependent. It is difficult to imagine strong relationships in a classroom where foundational routines have not been established. Conversely, it is challenging to imagine attention to routines without the development and strengthening of relationships. Both are needed and will benefit the learner and the learning environment greatly.

## REFERENCES

Ahlstrom, W. M., & Havighurst, R. J. (1971). *400 losers; Delinquent boys in high school*. San Francisco, CA: Jossey-Bass Publishers.

Covey, S. (1989). *The 7 habits of highly effective people*. New York: Simon & Schuster.

Hargreaves, A., & Fullan, M. (2013). The power of professional capital: With an investment in collaboration, teachers become national builders. *Journal of Staff Development*, pp. 36–39.

Jones, S. M., Bailey, R., & Jacob, R. (2014). Social-emotional learning is essential to classroom management. *Phi Delta Kappan*, pp. 19–24.

Morganett, L. (2001). Good teacher-student relationships: A key element in classroom motivation and management. *Education*, pp. 260–264.

Rogers, S., & Renard, L. (1999). Relationship-driven teaching. *Educational Leadership*, pp. 34–37.

Shiller, J. (2008). "These are our children!" An examination of relationship-building practices in urban high schools. *Urban Review*, pp. 462–485.

Witmer, M. (2005). The fourth R in education—relationship. *The Clearing House*, pp. 224–228.

*Chapter 2*

# The Importance of Developing Relationships and Routines

A review of the literature, which reveals the importance of relationships with students, families, and other school personnel will be explored further in this chapter. Research on the benefits of relationships will be cited through this study. We will also explore the use of routines through a variety of perspectives, including those of practitioners as well as families. The conversation will begin with an exploration of the literature on the importance of routines.

## CLEARLY ESTABLISHED ROUTINES

Ask any seasoned teacher about establishing clear routines and procedures. He/she will share that this is one of the most important tasks a classroom practitioner can engage in. To the educational veteran, clear routines can separate the best from the novices. Those who are regarded as great teachers look vastly different from those who aren't, and the ones who make the job look effortless are different from those who make it painful to watch them teach.

Establishing clear classroom routines and procedures is vital for ensuring that a classroom runs smoothly so that teaching and learning can take place. Routines, in a nutshell, provide the backbone of the effective classroom. Although they cannot exist in isolation without other essential elements, such as effective teaching and positive relationships, they are critically important. Routines, writes Denise Young, can nurture a sense of ownership and community in the classroom (http://www.learnnc.org/lp/pages/735).

The reader would be hard-pressed to find any discussion of effective classroom management that did not include a reference to the importance of establishing rules and procedures (routines). Evertson and Weinstein (2006) examined over fifty years of research, finding that the need for rules and procedures in the school environment was mentioned implicitly or explicitly in most of the literature reviewed (Evertson & Weinstein, 2006). Marzano (2003) reviewed over 100 studies, finding that establishing rules and procedures had an effect size of –0.76 with disruptive behavior (Marzano, 2003). Taken together, this examination of the literature clearly points the reader to the critical need for routine in schools and the potential impact on classroom management as well as on student behaviors and actions.

According to Ronald Partin (2005), "Establishing your hopes, expectations, rules, and routines is an essential first-day goal" (p. 9). Time spent in school is eroded through transitions and other scheduled activities, clerical tasks performed by teachers, ineffective instruction, and other inefficiencies (Partin, 2005). Attention to carefully chosen and implemented school routines can reduce the negative effects of time lost. The clarification of processes and procedures through explanation, demonstration, and practice helps get the year off to a smooth start.

Clear routines are not just beneficial to classrooms; they are important for bedtime, meals, getting up in the morning, and a variety of other routines and activities that children and students participate in during the day. In an article by Lisa Medoff (http://www.education.com/magazine/article/importance-routines-preschool-children/), she says that routines help eliminate the need for discourse because expectations for behavior are established. When behavioral expectations are clearly established, power struggles between adults and children are reduced or eliminated altogether.

In addition, routines help reduce stress for the adults involved. Implementing even small routines can have a sizable impact on the lives of children and adults. Other benefits of establishing routines include helping young people learn to take charge of their own activities, getting them on a schedule of predictability, helping adults build and maintain moments of closer connection with children, and assisting adults in maintaining consistency in expectations (http://www.ahaparenting.com/parenting-tools/family-life/structure-routines).

The American Occupational Therapy Association, Inc. (AOTA) has developed a tip sheet for establishing a morning routine for children. The detailed tip sheet provides a rationale as well as activities for a variety of morning routines. The AOTA suggests specific activities for getting children up in the morning, promoting a positive mood and behavior, preparing for morning demands, promoting participation and independence, and other critical behaviors (http://www.aota.org/About-Occupational-Therapy/Patients-Clients/ChildrenAndYouth/Morning-Routines.aspx).

Some teachers say that the most effective routines occur at the beginning of the class day or period. A simple search on the internet will yield templates, books, suggested apps, and workbooks for establishing the perfect morning routine for children from preschool through adulthood. There is no shortage of resources and ideas, all based on the premise that getting off to a good start is the key to having a successful day. Each of the authors have established routines that seem to work for them—Patty begins with yoga and meditation, Candice starts with a vigorous trip to the gym, and Todd swears by his cup of java and a hearty breakfast. A critical element in each of these activities is that everything is accomplished before 6:00 a.m. The routines vary, but the belief in their importance is shared by all.

Many teachers have an activity posted for students to begin working on as they enter the classroom. In these classrooms, students know the procedures because they've been taught to follow them, resulting in no time being wasted. Such morning routines establish an orderly, efficient atmosphere because students generally do not need to be directed as to what is expected. This also forces students to take responsibility; they know it is their job to get right to work.

Classroom routines don't just make life easier, they save valuable time. They make it easier for students to learn and achieve more. Successful teachers establish routines early in the academic year to facilitate the fluid and efficient flow of instruction (Leinhardt, Weidman, & Hammond, 1987). These researchers found that the major difference between expert and novice teachers was the use of well-practiced routines. Routines enable teachers to pace the practice and give rapid feedback on performance to all the students.

Routines also eliminate many potential disruptions and problem situations—for example, the common problem of getting the teacher's attention and help. Typically, students who need help must raise their hands, wait to be acknowledged by the teacher, state their needs, and then receive an oral directive. This very public request for help not only may embarrass some children or be used as a controlling mechanism by others; it disrupts the entire class every single time it occurs.

In an examination of classrooms that are managed effectively, Emmer, Everton, and Worsham (2003) suggest that it is impossible for teachers and students to work productively without guidelines for interactions with one another, including how students behave and how they move throughout the classroom (p. 17). Marzano, Marzano, and Pickering (2003) indicate that designing and implementing rules and procedures is one of the most obvious aspects of effective classroom management (p. 13). It stands to reason that carefully crafted routines for the implementation of rules and procedures ensure that classrooms are efficient as well as effective in fulfilling their purpose, educating the nation's youth.

Although there seems to be universal agreement on the importance of routines, there is not apparent agreement on what the "correct" or "best" classroom routines should look like. In an examination of classroom routines, Barbara King-Shaver suggests that teachers should use what works best in each individual classroom (http://www.scholastic.com/teachers/article/routines-and-procedures). Effective classrooms follow a variety of processes and routines, including bell-ringers to start class (http://www.brighthubeducation.com/teaching-methods-tips/85130-bell-ringer-activities-for-your-classroom/), strategies for working together cooperatively (Kagan & Kagan, 2009), and routines for ending the class period, such as the use of exit slips (Marzano, 2012) or Learning Expressways. Learning Expressways is a routine for giving and receiving feedback developed by the University of Kansas Center for Research on Learning (www.kucrl.org). Beginning and ending the class period is just one of many points during the day when routines are needed.

Routines are absolutely essential for the efficient and effectively managed classroom. They create a sense of calm order in which both adults and children thrive. Without well-established routines, much time is wasted and the potential for a chaotic climate is omnipresent. In the following section, we will examine the importance of relationships between students and their teachers. As stated earlier, relationships and routines are equally important. Both contribute to the classroom climate and culture in which optimum learning takes place.

## DEVELOPING RELATIONSHIPS WITH STUDENTS

In the first section of this chapter, the importance of establishing routines was emphasized. In this section, a close examination of teacher-student relationships will be conducted. Relationships will be examined in terms of their potential to generate positive student results as well as their closely linked bond with clearly established routines. According to Partin (2005), students entering the classroom have psychological, as well as learning, needs that lead them to wonder if they will be accepted, safe, and comfortable, all indications that relationships with others, including the teacher, are critical.

One can hardly think of previous teachers without remembering that special individual whose impact was deeply profound because it was known that, without a doubt, the teacher cared deeply about that child, that adolescent, that student. This teacher may have been tough, firm, or unyielding in some aspects, but underneath all of this was the human-to-human relationship as demonstrated by deep and abiding unconditional care and concern. As can be seen in the next few paragraphs, relationships are not just about having a positive rapport between teacher and student.

Well-established positive relationships can positively impact student achievement, discipline, a love of learning, and even the other relationships the student may be a part of. In short, there is no end to the potential that a well-developed student-teacher relationship can have. There is an old adage: children do not care what you know until they know that you care. These simple yet profound words are echoed in the work of Mark and Christine Boynton.

These authors suggest that all humans want to feel valued and cared for by those who hold significance in their lives (Boynton & Boynton, 2009). This truth is a powerful nugget of knowledge for the classroom teacher as he/she forms a blueprint for disciplinary procedures. The authors further assert that students need to know they are cared for and valued as individuals, and that this understanding leads to improved behavior. Listening to students and providing an empathetic caring climate both help convey to students that they are deeply cared for, according to Boynton and Boynton (2009).

Relationships provide the foundation for student acceptance of rules and procedures as well as consequential disciplinary action. In a meta-analysis for teacher-student relationships, Marzano found that the average effect size for teacher-student relationships was −2.891 for middle school/junior high and 1.606 for upper elementary students, suggesting that teacher-student relationships are extremely important to students (Marzano, 2003). In other related research, it was seen that discipline problems could have been avoided by better relationships between teachers and students (Sheets, 1994; Sheets & Gay, 1996). Each of these studies strongly suggests the power of the relationship between teachers and students.

In studies attempting to identify the characteristics of teachers who are more likely to have good relationships with students, some factors such as consideration and patience have been suggested (Good & Brophy, 1995). Wubbels (1999) has identified two dimensions whose interactions define teacher-student relationships. These two dimensions are cooperation versus opposition and dominance versus submission. In his research, Wubbels suggests that teachers need to be effective in both their delivery of instruction and their friendliness, helpfulness, and congeniality (Wubbels, 1999). In other words, the best teachers maintain classroom control while valuing the cooperation aspects of their practice.

Smith, Fisher, and Frey (2015) discuss the importance of building positive and trusting relationships with students while keeping, making, and building peace in the classroom. These authors refer to restorative practice, suggesting that teachers must work in concert with students to establish a respectful classroom climate. The implication that relationships and routines are positively intertwined is astoundingly evident. Even the name, *Better Than Carrots or Sticks: Restorative Practices for Positive Classroom Management*, directs the reader to understand that relationships are forever linked with routines. The authors make the case that the classroom that is welcoming, while at the same time enriching and constructive through a co-constructed approach, will result in student achievement (2015).

As suggested earlier, attention to relationships can result in greatly improved classroom practice. In short, positive student outcomes can be vastly enhanced through cultivation of genuine, caring relationships. Marzano, Pickering, and Heflebower (2011) discuss the importance of connecting to students' lives and their life ambitions as critical to creating a highly engaged classroom. Through careful attention to individual student characteristics and recognizing that "students have many goals that relate to learning" (p. 88), teachers can assist students as they make connections to students' personal goals through their instruction. In short, connecting with students helps students learn.

In a 2012 article from the *Education Week,* Kelley Clark identifies strategies that have the potential to cement strong relationships with students and may lead to them wanting to go above and beyond in their academic efforts. Clark suggests that teachers engage in the following practices:

1. Remind yourself to ask caring questions about students' lives, including family, sports, interests, and so on.
2. Respond to all students in ways that never call negative attention to them or any other student.
3. Use interest surveys and getting-to-know-you information in conversation with students.
4. During classroom activities, remember to insert opportunities to ask students questions about what they are interested in.
5. Learn to identify your students by name on the first day.

Clark, a high school math teacher, reminds the reader that teachers need to master their content as well as never forget to whom they are teaching that same content (Clark, 2012).

Another classroom strategy closely tied to building and maintaining positive relationships with students is cooperative learning. There are five defining elements of cooperative learning, according to David Johnson and Robert Johnson (1999). These elements include positive interdependence, face-to-face promotive interaction, individual and group accountability, interpersonal and small group skills, and group processing. The relationship-focused components can be readily detected through close examination of these elements. Trust, helping one another, working with others, and other skills are deeply embedded in cooperative learning as a classroom practice.

In their research on cooperative learning, Kagan and Kagan (2009) report that social skills are on the decline as a result of numerous factors including increased aggression and violence in the United States. The Kagans further assert that the need for positive relationships, including a focus on interpersonal skills, teamwork, flexibility and adaptability, and a sense of humor is on the increase (National Association of Colleges and Employees, 2004). The Kagans (2009) their case for teaching relationship skills through cooperative learning because:

> No one is consistently providing correction opportunities, helping children forge positive values and virtues. But students need a value system-rights and wrongs to guide their behavior. Lacking the traditional sources of guidance, today's youth is overly influenced by commercial pop culture and succumbs to peer pressures. Discipline and virtue are replaced by immediate gratification, lack of impulse control, competition, and aggression. (p. 14)

Although one can make the case that the Kagans have, perhaps, overgeneralized, the need for a focus on relationship development and strengthening is evident in their rationale. In short, cooperative learning strategies, which focus on positive teacher-to-student and student-to-student relationships, have been recognized as one of the best educational approaches (Ellis & Fouts, 1993) and one of the most flexible and powerful strategies in the classroom (Marzano, Pickering, & Pollock, 2001).

Establishing relationships with students that are positive and meaningful help ensure that students feel valued, cared for and safe, while also providing a climate in which students are more likely to follow established rules and procedures. Teachers who are effective in both instruction and cooperation have been demonstrated to be more effective than teachers where there is a lack of control in a less-caring environment. Involving students in establishing a culture that values every participant through jointly developing processes, as well as engaging in cooperative learning are pathways that result in a thriving classroom where all students are respectful and fully engaged in the learning process.

## FINAL THOUGHTS

In this chapter, the importance of well-established routines and strongly valued relationships has been explored. As noted, both are critical to the well-managed classroom. Students of all ages thrive in environments with highly defined yet humanely implemented procedures and processes coupled with trusting and caring relationships with both adults and other classmates. Foundational to any other instructional practices are the routines and relationships that support them.

The critical need for clearly established routines and well-developed, positive relationships, which has been demonstrated in this chapter, will be echoed as the reader is introduced in chapter 3 to the Interaction Congruence

Theory (ICT). The theory serves as foundation to the specific routines and strategies targeting the development and strengthening of relationships with students.

These specific routines and strategies have been crafted and refined over the last twenty years by Todd Scott Parker with hundreds of students through his work in inner-city urban as well as suburban school districts, both large and small. Collectively, these routines and relationship-strengthening strategies are called the Relationship Management System (RMS)™. These routines and relationship-focused strategies have been developed and utilized with students in grades K through 12 and have resulted in increased achievement and positive behavior. The specific strategies will be fully described in Section II.

## REFERENCES

Boynton, M., & Boynton, C. (2005). *Educator's guide to preventing and solving discipline problems.* Alexandria, VA: Association for Supervision and Curriculum Development.

Brown, E. (2015). School dropout study: 'You don't have to be Mother Teresa to help a kid.' Retrieved from https://www.washingtonpost.com/local/education/school-dropout-study-you-dont-have-to-be-mother-teresa-to-help-a-kid/2015/09/15/70ddb0c4-5b22-11e5-b38e-06883aacba64_story.html.

Clark, K. (2012). *Five practices for building positive relationships with students.* Retrieved from http://www.edweek.org/tm/articles/2012/08/07/tln_clark.html.

Ellis, A. K., & Fouts, J. T. (1993). *Research on educational innovations.* Princeton Junction, NJ: Eye on Education.

Emmer, E. T., Evertson, C. M., & Worsham, M. E. (2003). *Classroom management for secondary teachers* (6th ed.). Boston: Allyn & Bacon.

Establishing morning routines for children. (n. d.). Retrieved from http://www.aota.org/About-Occupational-Therapy/Patients-Clients/ChildrenAndYouth/Morning-Routines.aspx.

Evertson, C., & Weinstein, C. S. (Eds). *2006 Handbook of Classroom Management: Research, Practice, and Contemporary Issues.* Mahwah, NJ: Erlbaum.

Good, T. L., & Brophy, J. E. (1995). *Contemporary educational psychology* (5th ed.). White Plains, NY: Longman.

Johnson, D. W., & Johnson, R. T. (1999). *Learning together and alone: Cooperative, competitive, and individualistic learning* (5th ed.). Boston: Allyn & Bacon.

Kagan, S., & Kagan, M. (2009). *Kagan cooperative learning.* San Clemente, CA: Kagan Publishing.

Leinhardt, G., Weidman, C., & Hammond, K. M. (1987). Introduction and integration of classroom routines by expert teachers. Retrieved from http://www.jstor.org/stable/1179622.

Marzano, R. J. (2012). Art and science of teaching/the many uses of exit slips. *Educational Leadership (70)*2.

Marzano, R. J., Marzano, J. S., & Pickering, D. J. (2003). *Classroom management that works: Research-based strategies for every teacher.* Alexandria, VA: Association for Supervision and Curriculum Development.

Marzano, R. J., Pickering, D. J., & Heflebower, T. (2011). *The highly engaged classroom.* Bloomington, IN: Marzano Research.

Marzano, R., Pickering, D., & Pollock, J. (2001). *Classroom instruction that works: Research-based strategies for increasing student achievement.* Upper Saddle River, NJ: Pearson.

Medoff, L. (2013). Routines: Why they matter and how to get started. Retrieved from http://www.education.com/magazine/article/importance-routines-preschool-children/.

National Association of Colleges and Employees. *Job Outlook* 2004. Bethlehem, PA: National Association of Colleges and Employees, 2004. Retrieved from www.naceweb.org.

Partin, R. L. (2005). *Classroom teacher's survival guide: Practical strategies, management techniques, and reproducibles for new and experienced teachers* (2nd ed.). San Francisco, CA: Jossey Bass.

Positive parent-child relationships. (n.d.). Retrieved from http://eclkc.ohs.acf.hhs.gov/hslc/tta-system/family/docs/parent-child-relationships.pdf.

Rice-Linn, P. (2012). *You'll be saved by the bell-Ideas and activities.* Retrieved from http://www.brighthubeducation.com/teaching-methods-tips/85130-bell-ringer-activities-for-your-classroom/.

Routines and procedures. Retrieved from http://www.scholastic.com/teachers/article/routines-and-procedures.

Sheets, R. (1994, February). *Student voice: Factors that cause teacher/student confrontations in a pluralistic classroom.* Paper presented at the annual conference of the National Association of Minority Education, Seattle, WA (ERIC Document Reproduction Service No. ED371089).

Sheets, R. H., & Gay, G. (1996, May). Student perceptions of disciplinary conflicts in ethnically diverse classrooms. *NASSP Bulletin,* pp. 84–93.

Smith, D., Fisher, D., & Frey, N. (2015). *Better than carrots or sticks: Restorative practices for positive classroom management.* Alexandria, VA: Association for Supervision and Curriculum Development.

Why kids need routines & structure. Retrieved from http://www.ahaparenting.com/parenting-tools/family-life/structure-routines.

Wubbels, T., Brekelmans, M., van Tartwijk, J., & Admiral, W. (1999). Interpersonal relationships between teachers and students in the classroom. In H. C. Waxman & H. J. Walberg (Eds.), *New directions for teaching practice and research* (pp. 151–170). Berkeley, CA: McCutchan.

Young, D. (n.d.). *Classroom routines and procedures.* Retrieved from http://www.learnnc.org/lp/pages/735.

*Chapter 3*

# The Interaction Congruence Theory

Relatability is a crucial part of developing a culture of learning. In this chapter, you will learn about certain necessities that ensure all stakeholders contribute genuinely to this culture. These necessities need to be initiated by the leader or adult in the environment. A basis for establishing a culture of learning begins with understanding one's personality so that all parties experience genuineness when expressing themselves. Understanding the traits, characteristics, or even imperfections allows students to see the teacher—the adult—as human.

The Interaction Congruence Theory (ICT) was developed as a result of reviewing the literature on relationships, rapport, respect, and interactions primarily between students and others in school settings. Countless conversations with educators all reporting classroom management, interactions, and relatedness as the most challenging aspects of their teaching was also used anecdotally to conceptualize this theory. However, the theory is also applicable to other disciplines and settings.

Each author has been an educational leader in various capacities. Through their work, each has experienced situations of having to mediate conflicts between multiple individuals, especially teachers and students. A large portion of these mediations led to the conclusion that the personalities of the parties involved were not corresponding, or congruent. The lack of congruence could be attributed to young people who were displaying the signs and symptoms of being interaction deprived or the adults who experienced difficulty in acknowledging or accepting the ways in which student's expressed their personality traits. These experiences by the authors eventually laid the groundwork for the ICT.

Research asserts that young people of various demographic backgrounds perform better while interacting genuinely with the adults within the environment (Wubbels, 1999). In 1987, Leinhardt, Weidman, and Hammond concluded that routines established early in the school year greatly impact the fluidity and pace of the instruction. Therefore, successful teachers who set firm classroom expectations, practices, and routines increase the instructional opportunities in their classrooms because they are spending less time on behavioral management.

Additional research suggests that positive student outcomes are influenced and cultivated by genuine and caring relationships with teachers (Clark, 2012; Marzano, Pickering, & Heflebower, 2011). These relationships oftentimes motivate students to increase their academic effort and output. Relationships can be a powerful element in supporting the overall environment. If you closed your eyes and thought about that teacher who had a positive influence on your life, you might also recognize how this individual impacted your life like a concentric pattern. It is the understanding that their teaching and influence is branded and connected to many aspects of your professional and personal life.

In addition to the research on routines and relationships along with the countless conversations with practicing professionals, the authors also explored Charlotte Danielson's Framework for Teaching and the evaluation instrument. Many educators are familiar with the Danielson's framework that addresses four domains of effectiveness. Those domains are: Instruction, Classroom Environment, Preparation and Planning, and Professional Responsibility (Danielson, 2013; 2007). Domain Two of the Danielson framework addresses various elements of classroom environment.

The ICT expands many of the commonly identified environmental and classroom management elements to focus more specifically and more deeply on four components: Rapport, Responsiveness, Respect, and Routines. These components are reported by novice and veteran teachers as the most challenging and difficult to address in the classroom and school setting. One of the obvious reasons why relationship and classroom management is so incredibly difficult for teachers is simply the human factor.

Generally, teachers are highly knowledgeable about academic content. They can develop lessons. They understand how to assess and address the impact on student learning. They are proficient activity developers. However, it is arguably impossible to address every personality characteristic, action, behavior, attitude, and disposition that might impact instruction. Classroom management, behavior guidance, and relatedness are all influenced by a student's background, history, and culture. It requires a delicate balance to manage these elements effectively.

Therefore, classroom management does not always follow a literal, or even, a linear sequence of actions. It's fluid. It requires flexibility, patience, and consistency and, most of all, time and consideration of the humanity that is represented in the classroom. This delicate balance of relationship building, responding to cultural needs and applying consistent routines is essential to the equilibrium of interactions. The ICT accounts for those ideas and perspectives to focus on the relatedness elements that, when used effectively, can support the academic, social, and emotional learning.

This theory supports the implementation of the Relationship Management System (RMS)™ later explained in this book, to enhance the interactions between all members of the learning environment. When teachers are persistent in developing quality relationships with their students, discipline infractions decrease and student engagement increases. Students are also more inclined to be accepting of consequences and they are more likely to reflect appropriate adherence to classroom procedures (Marzano, 2003; Sheets, 1994; Sheets & Gay, 1996).

## INTERACTION CONGRUENCE THEORY (ICT) EXPLAINED

The ICT is comprised of five elements: Personality Package™, Rapport, Respect, Routines, and Responsiveness. These elements work in concert to support teachers in strengthening their level of classroom management effectiveness, as illustrated in figure 3.1. Each element will be explained in more detail below.

### The Personality Package™

The Personality Package™ is a process used to identify genuine characteristics, dispositions, and traits to express one's personality. The Personality Package will help one embrace how your characteristics and traits strengthen

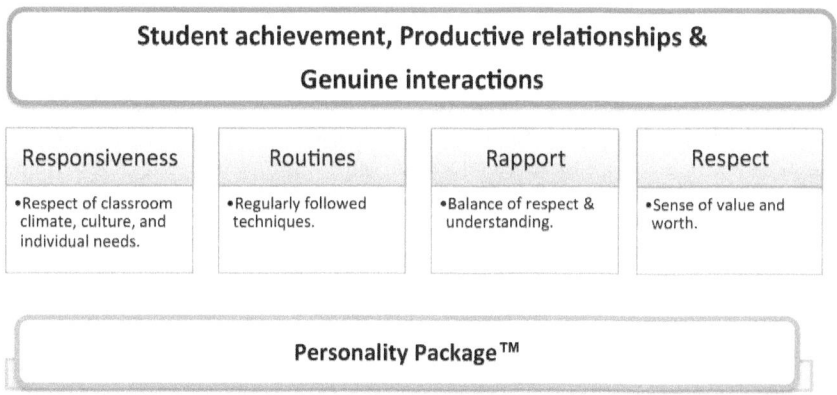

Figure 3.1    Interaction Congruence Theory (ICT).

the quality of interactions with others. For more information on the Personality Package™ and how to implement it in your school visit: www.parkeredanddevelopment.com.

## Responsiveness

Responsiveness is the ability to respond to changing conditions with respect to the culture and climate of the learning environment. A responsive teacher addresses the academic and social-emotional needs of all students. The teacher embraces and nurtures the cultural connectivity, even tempered responses, and social-emotional security within the classroom.

## Routines

Routines are regularly followed sequential actions and techniques. When implementing effective routines, the teacher should expect an increase in student engagement and instructional time, a decrease in misbehavior, and fewer disciplinary actions. Additional benefits are improved procedures, effective supervision, and a high functioning learning environment.

## Rapport

Rapport refers to the balance of respect and understanding that occurs between individuals. When building rapport the teacher acknowledges the various personalities, strengths, needs, and backgrounds represented in the classroom. The teacher recognizes his/her responsibility to create an environment that supports the delicate balance between group and individual needs. When a positive rapport has been established the teacher can expect the climate to be sustaining, for example, during a temporary absence, when a substitute teacher is present.

## Respect

Respect focuses on a sense of worth, value, and pride in one's performance and learning. Respect creates a sense of social and emotional security within the classroom. It also addresses character building that transcends the classroom. Additionally, respect supports an overall intentional culture of learning and expectations for, and of, success.

## FINAL THOUGHTS

To conclude, this theory possesses the primary elements to positively affect student achievement, maximize productive interactions, and manifest positive relationships. The implementation of the ICT is best delivered in a consistent manner. Each element can be reexamined and reintroduced throughout the school year and when interacting with students and others. The system of strategies that will be introduced in section II is aligned to the ICT and support teachers' and students' proficiency, effectiveness, performance, and interactions.

In the next chapter you will be introduced to the Alexander Crummell Academy. Throughout each of the remaining chapters, Crummell's story will emerge and unfold. As each chapter unfolds, the reader will learn more about the school, teachers, parents, and administrators. The reader will also learn, through Crummell's story, how the strategies are implemented in a real and authentic context.

## REFERENCES

Danielson, C. (2007). *Enhancing professional practice: A framework for teaching* (2nd ed.). Alexandra, VA: ASCD.

Danielson, C. (2014). The framework for teaching evaluation instrument. Retrieved from: www.danielsongroup.com.

Leinhardt, G., Weidman, C., & Hammond, K. M. (1987). Introduction and integration of classroom routines by expert teachers. Retrieved from http://www.jstor.org/stable/1179622.

Marzano, R. J., Marzano, J. S., & Pickering, D. J. (2003). *Classroom management that works: Research-based strategies for every teacher*. Alexandria, VA: Association for Supervision and Curriculum Development.

Sheets, R. (1994, February). *Student voice: Factors that cause teacher/student confrontations in a pluralistic classroom*. Paper presented at the annual conference of the National Association of Minority Education, Seattle, WA (ERIC Document Reproduction Service No. ED371089).

Sheets, R. H., & Gay, G. (1996, May). Student perceptions of disciplinary conflicts in ethnically diverse classrooms. NASSP Bulletin, pp. 84–93.

Wubbels, T., Brekelmans, M., van Tartwijk, J., & Admiral, W. (1999). Interpersonal relationships between teachers and students in the classroom. In H. C. Waxman & H. J. Walberg (Eds.), *New directions for teaching practice and research* (pp. 151–170). Berkeley, CA: McCutchan.

*Chapter 4*

# Meet Alexander Crummell Academy

In this chapter, the reader will be introduced to the Alexander Crummell Academy. This school, while fictional, is representative of numerous schools across the country. Crummell and its staff will be used throughout the book to demonstrate how to use the strategies and techniques in context. In subsequent chapters, the reader will have various opportunities to reflect on how staff have used the strategies effectively and/or ineffectively. The reader will also be provided with an opportunity to reflect on how these strategies might influence his/her practices.

Alexander Crummell Academy, a mid-size K–8 school in a large Midwestern city, was named after the famed abolitionist, theologian and founder of the American Negro Academy. He was born in New York to free parents in 1819. Later, Alexander Crummell became the first African-American graduate of Cambridge University. He was an advocate for African-American achievement in higher education and lived nearly twenty years in Liberia, before moving back to the United States.

The school always held great pride in representing such a pioneer in education. Each year the school would host The Alexander Crummell Day where students, teachers, and parents would celebrate the heritage and history of the school's namesake. They hosted College Day where teachers and students wore college paraphernalia—all to empower the students to pursue higher education. The debate team would host the Crummell Debate Show where students could present arguments regarding current sociopolitical issues and concerns. Everyone in the school was engaged and supportive of the various events associated with Crummell Day. Changes, however, impacted the school greatly.

Eight years ago, the community was considered a middle-class neighborhood where the median income was $125,000 for a family of four. Two income households were common. The neighborhood and surrounding community was somewhat racially and ethnically diverse. For three years, the school consecutively achieved or exceeded adequate yearly progress (AYP) in their district. Crummell was the district's shining star. Parent involvement was high. Teacher turnover was extremely low. There were a number of extracurricular activities and after-school programs for students. The school had experienced a great deal of success.

Over the last five years, the school, the district, and the community experienced many changes. Two of the largest employers closed. Nearly 30 percent of the families in the community worked for these companies. This caused significant financial hardship for many families in the community. The demographic landscape changed. The number of low-income families, many of whom were primarily African American and Latino moved into the community. Many of those families were seeking better opportunities and school systems. In other instances, families simply wanted their child in a higher performing school and exercised their right to school choice. All the while, the community was losing the affluent moniker it once had.

The community looked, felt, and operated differently. New families began to move in as old families moved out. The median income fell to below $65,000 for a family of four. Many new families moved into the community because of the school district's reputation for excellence. This only added to the increase in the student population and overcrowded classrooms. There was also a growing police presence in and around the school. Safety officers were hired to help control some of the community challenges—gang activity, drug dealing, and other crimes were on the rise. These challenges often spilled over into the school. Everything at Crummell was different and unfamiliar.

As a reflection of the community changes, Crummell also changed. The school moved from a K–6 to K–8 building. The achievement scores declined. There was a spike in detentions and expulsions. Many veteran teachers retired. The student population at Crummell grew from 365 students to 550 students. Thirty percent of the students were now receiving free or reduced lunch. This was quite indicative of the socioeconomic challenges the community was experiencing.

Budget cuts affected the extracurricular activities available to students in all schools. The cuts decimated Crummell's mentoring, dance, athletics, and all after-school programs and programming. Art and music were the only ones to escape cuts, in part due to a grant from a local theater philanthropist and jazz enthusiast.

Along with school changes, the district administration and school board were experiencing significant changes. A new superintendent was hired, only to leave after one year amid controversy. An interim superintendent was hired as his replacement. The new superintendent, Dr. Davidson, brought in her own staff, firing or reassigning many district administrators who had strong ties to the schools, the school board, and the community. She also implemented numerous other changes that further impacted curriculum, staffing, assessment, staff, and student morale—both positively and negatively.

As a result of the challenges with the district administration, the school board members were divided. Often times, the meetings were quite heated and unproductive. There appeared to be a great deal of infighting among board members. Many of the board members were allies of the outgoing superintendent and fought against the decision to bring in Dr. Davidson. Of the many charges leveled at Dr. Davidson, the most glaring was her lack of expertise, and knowledge about educational policies and financial management. There were rumors of irresponsible spending and favoritism for certain schools, especially those school where the board members' children were students.

## DEMOGRAPHIC CHANGES

Among the changes were the student demographics. There was a growth in African-American students from 30 percent to 50 percent. The Latino student population doubled to 30 percent. The once majority demographic, Caucasian students, decreased from 55 percent to 20 percent. The changes in the student demographic were starkly obvious. At times, the emerging demographics challenged the social and cultural context in the school. Many teachers found it difficult to relate and connect with students and families.

### Teaching Staff

Nearly half of the teachers retired over a three- to four-year period. However, the school staff, ranging from forty-two to forty-five members, remained diverse and with varied years of experience as shown below.

Approximately 55 percent of the teaching staff identified as female, 40 percent male, and 5 percent other. As a result of the mass retirement, there were only four teachers who remained at Crummell with more than ten years of

Table 4.1

| Years of Experience | % of Teaching Staff | African-American | Caucasian | Latino | Other |
|---|---|---|---|---|---|
| 1–3 | 35 | 25% | 55% | 15% | 5% |
| 4–6 | 42 | | | | |
| 7–10 | 15 | | | | |
| 10+ | 8 | | | | |

experience. This group, considered to be power brokers, had a great deal of influence and control within the teaching ranks, especially with the novice teachers. Often times these power brokers would disrupt and negatively impact potential progress.

The principal, whose career spanned thirty years, the last ten as the lead administrator of Crummell, retired. A new principal was hired as well as new teachers to replace those who'd retired. The new principal, Mr. Warren, was in his first year at Crummell. He was a fifteen-year veteran in education. He spent four years in the classroom as an eighth grade math and science teacher before moving into administration. Because of the success he'd experienced with turning the local high school around, he was moved to Crummell with the hopes of repeating that same kind of success. More of his story will emerge later.

## MRS. FRANKLIN: ASSISTANT PRINCIPAL

The assistant principal, Mrs. Franklin, was an African-American woman with eight years of experience. Five of her years were as a fifth grade science and math teacher. Her career started at Crummell. She was a mainstay—a fixture in the school. She had experienced and witnessed all of the changes at Crummell. While she made every attempt to remain positive, that effort was beginning to fade. More troubling was her dissent at being overlooked, yet again, and not being offered the principal's position at Crummell. She had good ideas for making improvements and questioned why she was not able to connect with, or convince others, that she was valuable.

Mrs. Franklin had been a great teacher. She was a respected administrator by most of the school personnel. However, she and Mr. Warren did not always see eye-to-eye on behavioral and disciplinary issues among students. Occasionally, the tension was palpable. He believed that she lacked the skills or fortitude to implement a structured school-wide behavior guidance plan. Moreover, when given specific plans to follow by Mr. Warren, those plans were met with opposition or not followed consistency.

This tension created unhealthy alliances among the school personnel. Some of the staff would refer to Mrs. Franklin as "Grandma Franklin" because she coddled students when they were misbehaving. Sometimes she would frustrate teachers and Mr. Warren because she would not hold students accountable for their actions when misbehaving. A part of her responsibilities was to implement a school-wide behavior and guidance program. She was failing miserably to implement a consistent and sustained program for all students.

## MR. LOCKLEAR: SPECIAL EDUCATION TEACHER

Crummell had experienced an increase in special education services by 25 percent. Moreover, Mr. Locklear, the new self-contained special education teacher for sixth through eighth grade, reported a sharp uptick of boys with social and emotional challenges being referred to for special education services. In fact, 12 percent of the students among the special education population were boys with social and emotional challenges. Many of the boys had been in special education classrooms for at least two years.

The previous special education teacher was highly effective in supporting the students, especially the boys. Most moved back to their regular classrooms within a year. Mr. Locklear hoped to have that same success. So far, he had managed to reach a few of the boys. He wanted so desperately to help his students feel successful and valuable.

Mr. Warren brought Mr. Locklear with him from the high school. Before becoming a teacher, he had worked for five years with boys and young men in the local juvenile justice system. Prior to that, he was the Youth Activities Director on his Native-American reservation. He enjoyed working in both his previous positions, but felt that he could have a greater impact in education, so he had changed careers. He found that what was most impactful with the boys and young men in his previous work was the relationships he built with them. Although he had connected with some of his students, not all were receptive. Some of the students were quite resistant and mistrusting of Mr. Locklear's efforts to get to know and understand them.

## MR. JUAREZ AND MISS GIOVANNI: COUNSELORS

A new male Latino counselor, Mr. Juarez, was hired to support the increase in Latino families in the community and school. Most of the new Latino families had extremely limited English. Mr. Juarez had spent much of his life in Mexico and moved to the United States when he was twelve. He graduated from the local high school and later from a nearby college. He knew and had grown up with many of the families. Before the after-school programs were defunded, he worked with the high school English teacher to teach English to the parents of the students. He wanted to help the families feel more connected with the school and teachers.

Crummell's other counselor, a Caucasian female, Miss Giovanni, also spoke Spanish. She was relieved when Mr. Juarez joined the staff. She was becoming overwhelmed with the amount of work and energy required to support many of the new Latino families. During her first three years at Crummell, she struggled to build relationships with many of African-American students and families who were apprehensive and mistrusting. She finally found a topic that helped her connect—sports.

She was a rabid basketball and football fan. She even coached the boys' team before the budget cuts rendered the athletic department obsolete. Now, she was looking for other ways to connect with parents. She had hopes of starting a parenting group to help restore the events and activities the school had once enjoyed—The Alexander Crummell Day being at the top of the list.

## MS. PRENTICE: FOURTH GRADE TEACHER

Ms. Prentice began her career four years ago at the height of the many changes affecting Crummell. She started as a second grade teacher, which she loved. For the past two years, she had been the fourth grade teacher, and was struggling. The district changed from a contained fourth grade to a departmentalized fourth grade last year. She was responsible for teaching social studies and literacy—two of the most challenging subjects for her students.

Last year's test scores indicated that nearly one-fourth of her students were reading below grade level. A few were advanced readers. However, most of those students felt social studies was boring. The other students were on target. Her major challenge was not teaching the content as much as her classroom management structure. She had more arguments among students, fights and other challenges than any other teacher in her grade level pod. Admittedly, this had always been a struggle for her. Ms. Prentice wanted to improve, but was not sure what to do. Last year it was so bad that the previous principal had a safety officer posted near her door, just in case she needed assistance.

This year was on track for being as problematic as the previous year. She already had two students suspended and one expelled. Ms. Prentice was considered a pushover by her students. They could "get away" with just about anything in her classroom. This sentiment was only made worse by the frustration she caused other teachers who, at times, had to step in the help her gain some control over her classroom. She was very timid, and sometimes, oblivious to the sights and sounds of the community that were reflected in her classroom. Clearly, Ms. Prentice has systemic issues with relationships and routines that needed immediate help.

## MR. WARREN: PRINCIPAL

Mr. Warren, introduced earlier, is the current principal of Crummell. When Dr. Davidson asked Mr. Warren to take over the school and bring it back to the level of prestige it once knew, he was ready for the challenge. Mr. Warren was highly revered for his no-nonsense approach to education. He was famous in the district for instilling an attitude among his staff, parents, and student body that success was the only option. He was a highly energetic and charismatic leader. His staff and students responded resoundingly to his enthusiasm.

His initial plan was to implement some structure into the school that would curb some of the discipline issues. He had also hoped to evaluate the school's data to determine where the gaps were. As a fifteen-year veteran in the district, the last ten years as the high school principal, he was not naïve about the challenges Crummell faced. He knew that it had been once revered. He knew that several teachers had retired and many of the current staff were fairly new. He expected the situation to be tough. What he did not expect was the climate and culture of the school to be so egregious in its violations.

## ALEXANDER CRUMMELL ACADEMY: PRESENT DAY

One day, Mr. Warren sat slouched behind his desk which was filled with mounds of assessment data from the first semester compiled into neatly organized stacks. He loved data, but with all of the discipline challenges, he had not had a chance to even review it. He gazed out of the window, while listening to his administrative team assemble in the conference room next door. They were begrudgingly preparing to spend their first professional development day (in September), combing through the data and brainstorming on what to do to bring up test scores.

Mr. Warren was perplexed. He was even disheartened by the lack of impact he had made to turn the school around thus far. He was even more bewildered by the lack of positivity and the disconnect between students, staff, and parents. What was even more disturbing and unexpected were the increasing behavioral and classroom management issues that were clearly related to the lack of relationship many teachers and other school personnel had with students.

He sighed as he spoke to the four walls of his office, "We've got to do something. There are too many teachers who just don't get it! Their interactions are poor and routines even worse. There's no real structure. The overall climate and culture is abysmal. The behavior and discipline strategies are inconsistent."

He shook his head while taking in a deep breath. He stood up, taking a few stacks from his desk, saying, "We've got to change this." He opened the conference room door and said, "Good afternoon, everyone. Let's get started."

He sat down at the head of the conference table placing the stacks of assessment data precariously on the razor's edge. His team looked on, waiting in an uncomfortable silence for Mr. Warren to speak again. He sat, for what felt like an eternity, mulling over the conversations he'd just had with himself in his office. His eyes darted toward the sheets of paper at the edge of the conference table. Suddenly, he realized that the data wasn't the issue at all.

As the realization of that epiphany washed over his face, he softened his furrowed brow. Looking up, he finally said, "The issue is not this data, ladies and gentlemen," slapping the stacks of paper. "The issue lies with the adults who are unprepared to work and interact with the young people in *this* school."

His team nervously glanced around the table at each other. Some narrowed their eyes in confusion. Others shifted nervously in their seats—folding their arms waiting for further explanation. Mr. Warren, feeling a burst of energy, rose from his seat. "So," Mr. Warren asked and he propped his palms against the table, "What are we going to do about that? What are we going to do help all school personnel develop better relationships with students, and what changes need to occur within the school's climate and culture to promote more positive routines in the classrooms? How are we going to make the necessary changes to ensure this school is once again producing students who are successful in life and learning? Those are the questions I want us to tackle today."

Even though Crummell had a few bright spots, it was a school in trouble. It was not the school it once was. There was no clear path toward success, and the esteem that the school had enjoyed was diminishing. The school's challenges were only made worse by the issues faced in the community. It is a story experienced by many teachers, students, parents, administrators, and communities across our country.

## FINAL THOUGHTS

Crummell's story will continue to unfold and deepen throughout each chapter. Other students and staff members will be introduced—all finding challenges and triumphs along the way, as they struggle to find success in and out of the classroom. This book will use Crummell's story to demonstrate how to use the presented strategies and techniques effectively for all K–12 learning environments.

The next section is the heart of the book. Chapters 5 through 8 will introduce the Relationship Management System (RMS)™. RMS is a system of strategies, techniques, and approaches designed to support positive interaction, student engagement, and relatedness. As mentioned in previous chapters, the system has been implemented, with success, in small and large districts in both urban and suburban communities.

Each chapter will present a component of the system and will follow Crummell's story, and its staff's implementation of the strategies. Each strategy is comprised of techniques that collectively make up the RMS™. This system has been implemented and proven to benefit adults with building productive relationships with young people, as well as relationships with other adults that work with young people. Section II will introduce the reader to the following strategies: Monitor 2 Modify, Relationship Management Pathways (RMP), D.E.P.T.H. Anchor, and lastly, P.R.P.L.E. Sandwich.

*Section II*

# INTEGRATING RELATIONSHIPS AND ROUTINES: THE RELATIONSHIP MANAGEMENT SYSTEM (RMS)™

The Relationship Management System (RMS)™ is a collection of strategies to support developing and strengthening the relationships and interactions and routines between teachers and students, and others, within the school context.

The graphic below illustrates how each of the strategies and approaches presented in this section fits together like a jigsaw puzzle. The reader will see the graphic used throughout section II to highlight the component of the RMS™ system that is represented in the respective chapter. For example, later in this chapter, the Monitor 2 Modify (M2M) puzzle piece will be highlighted.

Although each piece of the puzzle is complimentary to another, one may find a reliance on some strategies more than others depending on the character, climate, and culture of the school and classroom. Used together, however, the RMS™ system can enhance a school's existing behavioral guidance plan

Figure S2.1   Relationship Management System™ Diagram.

or can be implemented as the school's sole behavioral and discipline plan. The practices and procedures work to guide how students and adults interact, build relationships, and adhere to policies and protocols.

Below, figure S2.2 depicts the complete system of strategies, techniques, and approaches that comprise the RMS™. The authors encourage the reader to revisit the visual, when needed, to further conceptualize how the system works in concert to impact the school and classroom environment.

Each chapter in this section will continue Crummell Academy's story, representing how the teachers at Crummell Academy implement the strategy, both ineffectively and effectively. The reader will also have an opportunity to reflect on how the strategies might be implemented effectively into his/her practices, procedures, and classroom management systems.

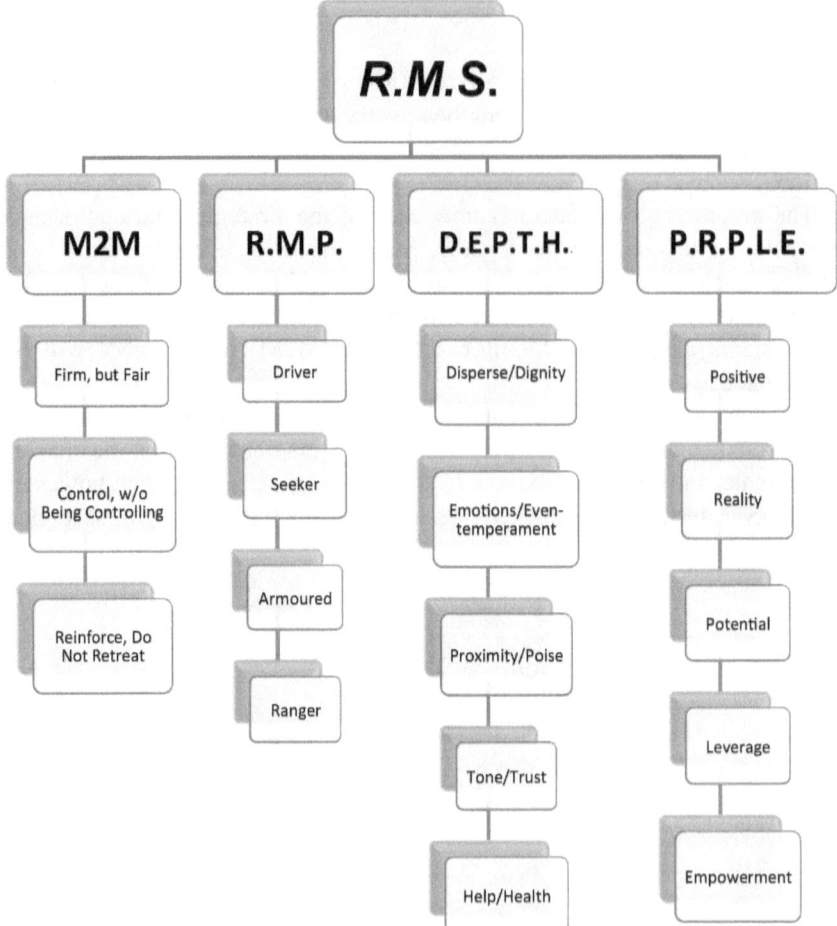

Figure S2.2   Relationship Management System™.

*Chapter 5*

# Monitor 2 Modify (M2M)

*Make time for routines early, or lose time without them all year long.*

*J. Smith*

As seen in figure 5.1, this chapter will explain the first RMS strategy, Monitor to Modify. Chapter 4 introduced you to Mr. Locklear, the special education teacher and Ms. Prentice, the fourth grade teacher. Mr. Locklear has found success in building relationships with some of the boys in his class, but is struggling with other students. Ms. Prentice who once was a second grade

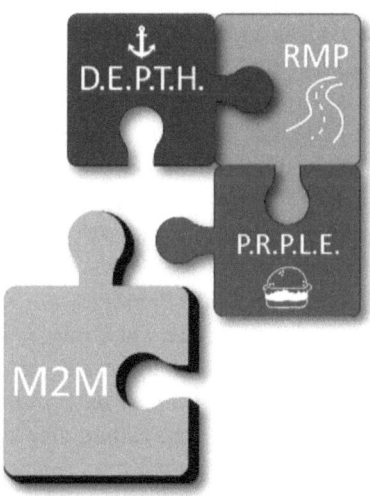

**Figure 5.1   RMSTM – Monitor to Modify (M2M).**

teacher, now a fourth grade teacher, is facing challenges, particularly with classroom management.

We will continue to examine Mr. Locklear and Ms. Prentice in various situations and scenarios. We ask the reader to engage in their dilemma or situation to gain a more authentic perspective of how Monitor 2 Modify (M2M) is used appropriately, and when the technique or routine is inappropriately implemented. Following the discussion of each routine, the reader will find an opportunity to think, reflect, and make connections to his/her own practices, procedures, and processes—components that might address school-wide policies or classroom expectations. Let's revisit Crummell and learn more about Mr. Locklear and Ms. Prentices' struggles.

*The week had been particularly challenging for both Mr. Locklear and Ms. Prentice. Mr. Locklear had trouble with many of the boys who had a history of exhibiting extreme behavioral challenges. He had squelched a few heated conversations between two of his male students over the last few days. He even had to intervene when a student in his first period class threw a chair across the room, narrowly missing another student. Plus, he had transitioned two new students into his class.*

*Additionally, Mr. Locklear was relentless in his attempts to break the ice with some of his students—students whom he knew had a wall up because of their backgrounds and circumstances. They were armored, as he had learned in a recent professional development workshop* (armored students will be addressed in detail in the following chapter). *While he now had a descriptor—a pathway—he still wasn't sure what to do to support them. It was a tough week for Mr. Locklear.*

*Ms. Prentice was drained and could not wait until the weekend to recover from her tough week. On Tuesday, she broke up a fight between two rival girls with the help of a nearby safety officer. On Wednesday, she had three uncomfortable conversations with parents and students about grades and the children's potential to be successful risk-takers. On Thursday, Mr. Warren, the principal, called her into his office to discuss complaints from other teachers that her classroom was out of control. Typically, these were the teachers who felt compelled to help Ms. Prentice, hoping to avoid potential altercations between students. However, they became weary of stepping into the role of being her rescuer.*

*It was Friday. Mr. Locklear and Ms. Prentice were sitting in the teacher's lounge, slouched in their seats, staring at, but barely touching their lunches—feeling tired and overwhelmed. It was a tough week. Ms. Prentice began sharing with Mr. Locklear what had happened over the past few days. As she talked, Mr. Locklear again thought about the professional development workshop from a couple of weeks ago on the Relationship Management System (RMS)* ™.

*From the workshop, he remembered learning about several strategies to support establishing positive relationships and routines. One of the strategies that he thought might be really helpful for both him and Ms. Prentice was M2M. He began conversing with Ms. Prentice about how they both might be able to use the strategy in their respective classrooms.*

## MONITOR 2 MODIFY (M2M) STRATEGY

M2M is a three-routine strategy designed to support teachers in strengthening their behavioral interventions for individual students, while continuing to honor the established classroom procedures, expectations, and/or school policies and procedures. The goal of this strategy is to ensure that students, teachers, parents, and administrators understand, adhere to, and respect the school and classroom procedures—procedures and expectations that ultimately support and positively impact student learning.

All of the strategies presented in this book are important and essential to developing relationships and routines with young people in school settings. However, the Monitor 2 Modify strategy sets the foundation for the RMS™. This strategy supports each component of the Interaction Congruence Theory (ICT) introduced in chapter 3. Responsiveness, rapport, respect, and routines are all based on how a teacher monitors the classroom environment and modifies their practices to appropriately address misbehavior and to promote desired behaviors.

This strategy is foundational to the relatedness and interactions between student and teacher. When engaged effectively, this strategy should:

- Support the development of positive relationships with students.
- Promote an intentional and productive culture of learning in the school.
- Foster a climate of respect, trust, and personal responsibility in the classroom.
- Enhance school-wide behavior guidance plan or disciplinary action policies.

M2M includes three distinct routines that work in collaboration to create a positive and productive learning environment. These routines are:

- *Firm, but Fair.*
- *Control without being Controlling.*
- *Reinforce, do not Retreat.*

In the next section, the first routine of this strategy—*Firm, but Fair*—is explained. The reader will learn what the routine is, why being firm, but fair is essential, and how to use the strategy effectively. We will also revisit Alexander Crummell Academy and its staff in several example scenarios.

## FIRM, BUT FAIR

*Firm, but Fair* is defined as having unwavering consistency of expectations, procedures, and rules. It includes implementing impartial behavioral guidance or consequences collectively and individually, as needed, or appropriate for the infraction. This routine is critical to a smooth functioning classroom and the development of procedures and consequences when warranted. In fact, it is difficult to establish or reclaim a positive classroom environment if a firm tone is not set early, and sometimes, revisited often.

Let's first examine the two aspects of tone that will be defined in this and subsequent chapters. First, setting a firm tone, not a punitive tone, in a classroom or school building should be established in the beginning of the school year. This is an important distinction, because many teachers believe that you need to be harsh or mean in order to control student behavior. The authors suggest that firmness simply means being consistent, resolute, and strong. For example, if a teacher is determined to ensure that his/her students learn the value and benefit of demonstrating compassion, then setting an unwavering, strong—*firm*—expectation of compassion is key. Therefore, tone in this regard refers to the overall attitude or character of a classroom or school—not voice volume or harshness.

Second, there is the tone of voice. The authors will go into greater detail about voice tone in chapter 7. However, for the purpose of this discussion, maintaining a voice tone that is lower than your speaking voice, is most effective. Additionally, ensuring that there is not an inflection at the end of the sentence that would signify a question makes your tone more credible—more decisive.

While there may be elements of voice tone when implementing this routine, *Firm, but Fair*, affirms the overall attitude and character set in a classroom and school. For example, you may work in a school where the tone, the attitude, and character of the classroom is one of excellence. If a student who has struggled with a concept for a long time finally gets it, your celebration may cause your voice tone to rise in exuberance. Certainly, this is acceptable.

To recap, while there are two types of tones, firmness and voice, this routine, *Firm but Fair*, focuses on establishing the classroom character or attitude of unwavering expectations of excellence and success. This will accomplish three things:

- Create a sense of respect for learning and desirable behaviors.
- Support the idea that all citizens are responsible for creating a classroom climate that is conducive for learning and academic success.

- Avoid the appearance of favoritism or victimizations. It is no secret that teachers, at times, will identify their favorite student or a student whose history evokes a sympathetic response. Either action can negatively impact the classroom environment and may create a sense of distrust between other students and the teacher.

*Firm, but Fair* is the frequency that vibrates throughout the school culture. It is modeled by all the adults—the teachers, support staff, counselors, and administrators. Establishing a firm tone does not allow for inconsistencies—inconsistencies that could dismantle or sabotage the structure and behavior guidance systems established in the school.

While maintaining a culture of firmness and a climate of personal responsibility, it is important to remain *fair*—impartial—in implementing disciplinary action or consequences for misbehavior. However, being fair also means that you are impartial when students are demonstrating desired behaviors. For example, Ms. Prentice shows the same steadfast impartiality to John, her favorite student, as she does Roman, her raucous student, when they both misbehave.

Similar to the idea that firm *is not* punitive, fair *is not* always equal. One misconception of being fair is that a consequence for a particular infraction will modify *any* student's behavior. This is simply not true. Ensuring that you remain consistent in redirecting a student's attention to expectations, while implementing an objective consequence for an infraction, is essential to maintaining a sense of trust, rapport, and respect in the classroom. Essentially, students know what to expect. The routines are consistent. The consequences are fair.

## Making Connections: *Firm, but Fair*

The following examples will illustrate when the *Firm, but Fair* routine is used ineffectively as well as effectively. They demonstrate how to use *Firm, but Fair* effectively to bolster consistent and positive behaviors, and adherence to expectations and procedures throughout the school setting. Let's go back to Crummell Academy.

*It was mid-September at Crummell Academy. Alexis was reprimanded for insubordination with a first level (Tier 1) consequence, Friday after-school detention. Alexis did not serve this detention. She chose to attend her after-school tutoring session to maintain her GPA so that she could remain on the basketball team. In response, Mrs. Franklin, the assistant principal who was also responsible for discipline, decided to remove Alexis from the basketball team for the entire season. She was happy to do so, as Alexis had earned the reputation of being a "mean girl."*

## How Does This Scenario Reflect *Ineffective* Implementation of *Firm, but Fair*?

Insubordination has been established as unacceptable within Crummell's rules and expectations. Alexis has engaged in an unacceptable behavior and will have to incur the consequences of that behavior. However, instead of Mrs. Franklin applying an objective consequence for Alexis, she unfairly removes her from the basketball team for the entire season. In this scenario, while Alexis may have some troublesome characteristics, Ms. Franklin's action could be perceived as harsh and not objective.

## What Would Have Been a More *Effective* Implementation of *Firm, but Fair*?

If serving Friday after-school detention was in conflict with her tutoring, Mrs. Franklin could have required her to serve a detention during lunch, PE, or perhaps sit out the first quarter of her next basketball game. The next scenario is more specific to typical occurrences in the classroom environment. It will illustrate another example of ineffective implementation of the *Firm, but Fair* routine.

*It was early October and Ms. Prentice was making a valiant effort at demonstrating firmness with her fourth grade class. However, Ms. Prentice was modeling to her students that sense of being overly fair to her "sweet" students. Carlos, who typically sat quietly in the back of the room completing his work, crumbled a piece of paper into a ball, stood up, and shot the paper ball into the trash can from across the room. "Swish!" he said. He did this while Ms. Prentice was in the middle of teaching a math lesson. Ms. Prentice stopped talking and asked Carlos to sit down without addressing the infraction.*

*Another student, James, blurted out with disdain, "Wow, Ms. Prentice! I did that last week and you sent me to the principal's office!" James was consistently reprimanded for his misbehavior and had incurred multiple consequences. She replied, "Yes. I did. But, Carlos doesn't do that as much as you do, James." Consequently, throughout the week, other students, who rarely misbehaved, began shooting paper balls into the trash can. This was not the proper procedure that Ms. Prentice established for her students when discarding paper. Regardless of who committed the offensive, the consequence should be fair, just, and unbiased.*

## How Does This Example Illustrate *Ineffective* Implementation of *Firm, but Fair*?

In this instance, Ms. Prentice was fair, but not firm. How? She unknowingly gave students permission to engage in this particular misbehavior by not addressing the classroom procedures for discarding paper. She also did not effectively address Carlos' behavior as she had done with James, who admittedly had engaged in the same misbehavior.

## What Would Have Been a More *Effective* Implementation of *Firm, but Fair*?

Ms. Prentice was thoughtful in attempting to be fair to Carlos' first infringement of the procedures. However, she should have taken that opportunity to firmly reiterate the procedure for discarding paper for all students, and perhaps, the consequences of repeated infractions.

## Think. Reflect. Connect.

Think of a time in your classroom or school in which a student or students have misbehaved. Reflect on the following questions:

- How did you address the misbehavior?
- How might the *Firm, but Fair* technique have helped you maintain your classroom management effectiveness?
- What, if anything, could you have done differently to ensure that you were both unyielding in expectations and unbiased toward the student or students?
- What evidence would affirm a positive outcome for the student or students if *Firm, but F*air was used effectively in your situation?

The technique of being *Firm, but Fair* constitutes an unwavering expectation of the procedure or practice, while promoting a sense of respect for fairness. No matter the number of times a particular routine is repeated, a firm, consistent delivery of that technique becomes a routine that promotes the idea of students holding themselves accountable for the culture and climate established in the classroom. It also provides the teacher with a reference point to ensure that the classroom is managed effectively. The next section will further define the *Control, without being Controlling* technique.

## CONTROL, WITHOUT BEING CONTROLLING

This technique requires additional context to fully conceptualize how the classroom environment can be influenced by the teacher's desire to exert control, his/her personality characteristics and traits, and the establishment of routines and practices. First, let us explore the difference between a controlled environment and a controlling environment.

A controlled environment supports a healthy culture of learning, while holding everyone in the environment accountable for the expectations, practices, and procedures therein. Let's continue with the example of a teacher establishing a routine or practice for how students should discard paper into the garbage can. Let's assume that students may have repeatedly practiced this routine and understand that they are to raise their hand for permission to walk to the garbage can to discard their paper. If a student gets up and shoots a ball of paper from across the room, he/she is making a choice to disregard that routine. So, how should the teacher set or reset the desired behavior or action?

The teacher can redirect the student, revisit the routine, and/or request that the student correct his/her action. In a controlled classroom environment, the student and teacher are both empowered to:

- Engage in self-discipline and problem-solving strategies.
- Maintain a respectful relationship that honors each person's status.
- Take meaningful action to engage in behaviors and activities that support the overall culture of learning.
- Be respectful, productive citizens of the classroom community and accountable for the established expectations, practices, and routines that guide the classroom climate and culture. This is paramount.

In contrast, a controlling environment is when a teacher inserts him/herself into every circumstance or situation that occurs in the classroom, regardless of its relevance. For example, instead of the teacher establishing a routine, having students practice the routine, encouraging students to self-correct, the teacher attempts to control all aspects of the students' behavior. In a controlling environment students are often led by a *helicopter teacher*.

A helicopter teacher tends to operate much like helicopter parent. The helicopter teacher becomes the "fixer" of problems, instead of the facilitator of problem-solving strategies. In these situations, students' social and emotional development can be impaired because the teacher is doing most of the thinking, working, and processing for the student. The student becomes a passive participant in the learning environment. Creating a culture of passive learning and participation may negatively affect the overall climate. This is simply unhealthy for the classroom environment and for students' learning.

A controlling teacher might make two walk-throughs of the classroom collecting students' work. This kind of activity wastes valuable instructional time. Sometimes a controlling teacher can paralyze students' growth and maturity, and could potentially cause greater classroom management challenges over time. Therefore, *Control, without Being Controlling* is a technique where the teacher and students work together to establish routines, procedures, and practices that lay a foundation for expectations, and positive behavioral and academic outcomes.

There are generally six concepts to consider when engaging this strategy:

1. Establish procedures and routines early. This might also mean developing procedures continually to address issues as they arise.
2. Apply consistent follow-through and repetition of the routine. This is especially true after long holiday breaks.
3. Redirect student, when necessary.
4. Engage consequences, when needed and appropriate. Maintain consistency when implementing a consequence.
5. Praise when the routine and procedures are followed consistently.
6. Focus on what students are doing right, as much or more than, what they are doing wrong. The goal should be to focus on positive behavioral guidance.

At a certain point within the school year, regardless of the age or grade, students have to eventually accomplish tasks independently. Whether these tasks are related to academic performance or social-emotional learning, independent practice allows them to see what success looks like, how to achieve their success, how to be graceful risk-takers, and how to celebrate small victories. These victories or achievements, can begin with classroom routines that will support, and ultimately, bolster academic success and performance.

Implementing the routines and procedures for students to perform within the first two months of the school year is helpful. That is not to say that implementing these strategies five months into the school year will not hold some benefit. During this time, however, the teacher would need to model, rehearse, and reiterate each of these procedures and routines with vigor and a high degree of consistency.

It may become a tedious task, yet the long-term goal is for the teacher to address the inappropriate behavior verbally, or with minimal redirection. In addition, as new misbehaviors occur, alternate procedures or new procedures may be developed to support behavioral challenges. This permits teachers to pick their battles wisely, instead of attempting to confront or anticipate all inappropriate behaviors.

## Making Connections: *Control, without being Controlling*

We revisit Crummell Academy to reflect upon ineffective and effective implementation of *Control, without being Controlling*. Ms. Prentice will be challenged by student behaviors during her lesson in this scenario.

*In mid-November the procedure for math transition in Ms. Prentice's class was for students to sharpen their pencils before moving their chairs to the designated math whiteboard. Some horseplay began at the sharpener due to the line forming when William complained about the sharpener not working. Ms. Prentice walked over to the sharpener and attempted to minimize the line by sharpening each student's pencil. Meanwhile, at the whiteboard, Katherine and Paula bickered over the same chair, which suddenly escalated into shoving. Ms. Prentice tried to intervene by running over to the whiteboard to separate the girls.*

## How Does This Scenario Reflect *Ineffective* Implementation of *Control, without being Controlling*?

Ms. Prentice devoted all of her attention to the situation at the pencil sharpener, while two other students' behavior escalated into misbehavior. She felt that solving the sharpener issue herself would alleviate the horseplay, but instead it altered her proximity to the whiteboard and gave rise to the potential for students to misbehave. Proximity would have allowed her a wider view of the classroom and might have given her the opportunity to address Katherine and Paula's behavior before it escalated. Even though students are following the transition procedure, her desire to control a hiccup in one procedure led to a different, more serious disruption in another area.

## What Would Have Been a More *Effective* Implementation of *Control, without Being Controlling*?

A quick analysis of possible electric pencil sharpener mishaps would have prompted Ms. Prentice to consider alternatives, while approaching the pencil sharpening area. One, Ms. Prentice could have surveyed the students at the sharpener to appoint the most qualified individual to remedy the situation. Two, remembering the general ideas presented earlier, she might have reminded students of the routines, in the hope they would self-correct. Either solution or decision would have been an initial proactive measure prior to. This would have allowed her to use proximity control to respond to the other students engaging in a potentially dangerous situation. How might you have used, *Control, without being Controlling* to respond to this situation? Let's explore another scenario.

*Mr. Locklear had a group of eighth grade male students within his self-contained special education class, who often did whatever it took to avoid doing classwork. On this particular day, Mr. Locklear wanted his students to remove their journal entries from their spiral notebooks to submit. The classroom erupted with lots of noise and complaints from students that tearing the pages at the perforated edge couldn't be done. Mr. Locklear abruptly ceased the lesson and told all students with difficulty with their journal to approach his desk. All at once, they noisily approached. He meticulously tore the sheet from each spiral notebook. This took seventeen minutes of his forty-five minute class period. Minutes later, the bell rang, class was dismissed, and only a portion of the lesson for that class period was implemented.*

## How Does This Scenario Reflect *Ineffective* Implementation of *Control, without being Controlling*?

Mr. Locklear commenced with controlling every aspect and situation occurring in his class—the beginning, the obstruction of, and the resolution to, this simple task. This is a self-contained classroom, and there may be students who may genuinely need Mr. Locklear's assistance. Remember this is also a group 8th grade boys, who try various tactics to avoid work. In the scenario, Mr. Locklear inserted himself as the students' problem-solver—fixer—instead of using it as a teachable moment to revisit the routine to help them learn how to be accountable to the classroom climate.

## What Would Have Been a More *Effective* Implementation of *Control, without being Controlling?*

With genuine relationships already established in the classroom setting, Mr. Locklear could have assessed the ability of his students to take detailed instruction for completing a task like tearing paper from a spiral notebook. In addition, he could have saved the task itself until the end of class that day, or the beginning of class the next day. For some students, especially the group of male students avoiding classwork, taking advantage of teachable moments to solve problems may curb future classroom management complications.

## Think. Reflect. Connect.

Think of a time in your classroom or school in which a task, or multiple tasks, were occurring all at once. Tasks can range from academic problem-solving to menial housekeeping tasks. Reflect on the following questions and make connections to your practices and procedures.

- What technique did you use to maintain control of the environment, without being controlling?
- How effective was the technique in maintain control?
- What could you have done differently, based on what you've read about *Control, without being Controlling*, which would have helped you be more effective?

## REINFORCE, DO NOT RETREAT

The last technique of the Monitor 2 Modify strategy is *Reinforce, Do Not Retreat*. When consequences are administered, the follow-through of those consequences has to be reinforced the year round. This may be especially challenging for new and novice teachers, who are often times in survival mode for much of their first one to two years in the classroom. Therefore, it is important to approach the beginning of the school year like one might build a house. A new house is built on a firm foundation, a firm structure. After the house has aged, settled, and so on, perhaps a crack appears in the foundation requiring that you add some type of reinforcement. In a classroom, a teacher implements a firm structure and tone in a controlled environment. Tone was defined and explored earlier in the chapter.

Eventually, students will begin testing that structure, firmness, fairness, and control. It is the teachers' responsibility, then, to reinforce the routines, or administer consequences for those students who consistently and unexpectedly engage in negative or disruptive behaviors. Hence, you must consistently *Monitor 2 Modify* your environment and students' behavior. This will help to ensure that accountability for the learning environment being maintained.

As the teacher monitors the classroom culture, it is important to avoid becoming paralyzed by one's own emotion, or the emotionality of students. The fact is, young people generally do not welcome facing the consequences for their misbehavior. If you issue a just consequence, do not retreat or succumb to your emotion or theirs. Be strong and resolute in your action and decision. Resist allowing their emotions or yours to interfere with the classroom management decisions. Create a safe and secure environment that students can come to trust and respect.

Teachers are human beings, of course. Therefore, getting it right all the time is almost impossible. However, there needs to be firm boundaries set for young people to respect in the classroom. Again, the objective is to maintain a culture of learning for all. Once boundaries are established, there may be a number of young people attempting to stretch or test those boundaries. Retreating from the consequences issued for misbehaviors or infractions may weaken the firm structure and the controlled environment, causing a domino effect.

If these boundaries are not solidified early and often, young people can quickly grow into an intolerable number of young people engaging in inappropriateness that eradicates the boundaries and creates disequilibrium within the classroom culture. Therefore, *Reinforce, do not Retreat* allows the teacher to support the positive environment without allowing his/her emotions to cloud decisions. Creating a positive environment with the firm, fair tone, and clear routines can support overall learning. Regardless of the lack of resources, human support, or likability of the student, the giver of that particular consequence cannot retreat.

Certainly, the follow-through is not always as easy as it sounds. If it were, classroom management and misbehavior would not be the great challenge teachers report it to be. Stepford children do not exist. A teacher cannot expect a student to immediately and forever behave appropriately at all times. However, with an intentional focus on relationship and routines, a teacher can establish an environment conducive to learning. Let's explore how Mr. Locklear uses this technique.

*As the speech team sponsor, Mr. Locklear felt the pressure from the administration to bring home a trophy with Michael, a star orator. Unfortunately, two weeks prior to the November speech regionals, Michael and two other students were caught stealing from the school bookstore. As the speech team rules stated, any major disciplinary infraction would result in a one event suspension. The rules allowed him to attend practice and competitions, but he had to sit and watch. Michael decided to skip practice and the next speech competition. Mr. Locklear inserted him into the next competition, despite the jeers from the rest of the team.*

## How Does This Scenario Reflect *Ineffective* Implementation of *Reinforce, do not Retreat*?

To many, Michael just not showing up for the next two events was enough of a consequence. However, due to the pressure that Mr. Locklear was feeling from administration, he decided to retreat to increase his chances of victory. This hinders the positive relationship between him and his team. It especially sends the wrong message to Michael, who could develop an invincibility complex with such a major infraction as stealing. It also ensures that other students, and possibly parents, will refer to this occurrence to avoid any major consequences in the future.

## What Would Have Been a More *Effective* Implementation of *Reinforce, do not Retreat*?

Extracurricular activities are prime opportunities to reinforce the disciplinary tone that has been established. In spite of the administration's pressure to excel at the speech competition, Mr. Locklear should have followed through with making Michael sit out the very next event he attended. Even though he was a star participant, sacrificing a potential award only strengthens the relationship with Michael and other participants for the future. Reinforcing and not retreating may even motivate other orators to work harder to become the next high achiever.

**Think. Reflect. Connect.**

Think of a time in your classroom or school when you were hesitant with reinforcing expectations, rules, procedures, or consequences. Explore the following questions and reflect on how the *Reinforce, do not Retreat* might improve or enhance your classroom or school culture.

- What compromise did you use to gain something or avoid being the *bad guy*?
- How effective was this compromise or technique?
- What might you have done differently to ensure the reinforcement of the culture was upheld?
- How would *Reinforce, do not Retreat* have supported your efforts?

## FINAL THOUGHTS

M2M is the first strategy presented as a part of the RMS™. It is comprised of three techniques to support a culture of learning—*Firm, but Fair*; *Control without being Controlling*; and *Reinforce, do not Retreat*. Together these techniques address the firm, but fair tone you set in your classroom to ensure all students are accountable for, and to, the environment. These techniques also empower the teacher and students to maintain a controlled classroom environment where *all* students can learn. Finally, reinforcing the routines, and the established consequences, will ensure that the classroom climate and the culture for learning are not sacrificed when students push or agitate boundaries.

In the next chapter, the reader will explore the common pathways, routes that people, especially young people, use to interact and connect with others. While the authors have identified four pathways, the authors acknowledge that more pathways may emerge and develop over time. Again, the authors will offer various opportunities to reflect on the pathways and how to use these pathways effectively. Ms. Prentice and Mr. Locklear will guide the reader on how the pathways can be used in combination with the first strategy—*M2M*.

*Chapter 6*

# Relationship Management Pathways (RMP)

*Effective teachers know how to teach, to the students they know.*

*C. Barnes*

As seen in figure 6.1, this chapter will introduce the reader to the Relationship Management Pathways (RMP). As defined in chapter 1, a pathway is a route, or a specified way in which interaction deprived students engage with others positively as well as negatively. Interaction deprived students

Figure 6.1 RMSTM – Relationship Management Pathway (RMP).

are those who have experienced a lack of reciprocal benefits of human relatedness. Relatedness is underscored by rapport, routines, relationship, and responsiveness.

Some may seek to fill the void by making incessant attempts to gain a teacher's attention. Others may attempt to call attention to themselves by challenging the routines and practices that guide the classroom management system. Students oftentimes develop these pathways based on their backgrounds, histories, and motivations, which depict how they interact with others and the depth to which they engage in their cultures of learning.

Still other students may shut down, bail out, or disengage from the classroom instruction or the classroom culture all together. There are others who demonstrate characteristics of multiple pathways that paralyze their learning and impact their interactions with others. It is important to note that these pathways are not strategies to implement in the classroom. The pathways are, however, lanes that students may maneuver when clamoring for attention. In the previous chapter on Monitor 2 Modify (M2M), Mr. Locklear noticed that at least one of his students was armored. As he thought about his other students, he began to identify those students who exhibited characteristics of driver, seeker, and ranger pathways.

Chapter 6 will delve further into each of those pathways. We will once again revisit Mr. Locklear and Ms. Prentice's efforts to effectively address the students identified as demonstrating the four pathways. The four pathways will be explored in scenarios that illustrate ineffective and effective approaches with each scenario. The reader will also have an opportunity to reflect upon the ways to engage and interact with individuals exhibiting characteristics of these pathways from a more general perspective. First, let's revisit Crummell and catch up with Mr. Locklear and Ms. Prentice.

*After implementing the M2M strategy, Mr. Locklear and Ms. Prentice saw some improvement in their students' behaviors, social interactions, and learning engagement. Initially, the students were slightly resistant. However, both teachers stayed the course in implementing the strategies. After a few weeks, they saw a significant change. Now, as Mr. Locklear began identifying the pathways that many of his students were using to interact with him and their peers, he decided to share that information with Ms. Prentice. His hope was that by sharing this information he might help her develop better relationships with her students and build more effective routines in her classroom.*

*After Mr. Locklear shared the information, Ms. Prentice began taking an inventory of her students in an attempt to identify who her drivers, armored, seeker, and ranger students were. Once that was established, she thought, "What do I do now?" She and Mr. Locklear discussed more of what he had learned in the professional development workshop about RMPs. They met after school to discuss ways to create a more specific plan for working with students who wanted to drive the class, those who were seeking attention at all cost, those students reluctant and hesitant to open up, and those students who exhibited behaviors of multiple pathways.*

*Mr. Locklear shared how he might handle those situations and students. Ms. Prentice shared her reservations and hesitancy in using his approach for fear that it might not come across as authentic to her personality. They talked through what might be the best way for her to respond to the needs of the students and the classroom, while making sure that she was also honoring her temperament and personality.*

*Ms. Prentice shared a few stories and situations. She worked with Mr. Locklear on affirming the most accurate pathways, given the descriptions that he provided. They talked through what might be the best way for her to respond—what language and tone she should use that would be most authentic. She realized that it was important to remember that her temperament and personality was essential to the believability factor and critical for student buy-in.*

*Still, she was concerned that even though there had been some positive changes, there remained questions about her ability to handle situations where students might require a more intensive strategy. As she discussed her tentativeness, Mr. Locklear immediately thought about how he had used D.E.P.T.H. Anchor to deescalate an intense situation he recently experienced in his classroom with a few students.*

D.E.P.T.H. Anchor will be discussed in more detail in chapter 7. For now, the reader will be introduced to the various pathways and routes that students travel in their attempt to engage and interact with others in their school and classroom environments.

The next sections will explain each of the commonly identified pathways and how teachers can work with those students effectively and genuinely to empower them to optimize the learning environment. This makes the strategies more operational and supports the culture of learning in and out of the classroom. This chapter will provide a description of the pathways. Then, scenarios will illustrate how the teacher approached the situations ineffectively, and, finally, how to approach the scenario effectively. Later the reader will have an opportunity to *reflect, think,* and *connect* on a deeper level of understanding how to engage with such interaction deprived students.

## RELATIONSHIP MANAGEMENT PATHWAYS

Young people have to endure life's ebbs and flows just like adults. Their experiences, backgrounds, culture, language, customs, and values play a huge role in their relatedness, student achievement, and success. Students bring those experiences into the classroom just as teachers will also bring their experiences into the classroom. As adults, however, we have the responsibility to guide students along the proper trail, or pathway, toward success. And while success will look different for each student, it should always be the goal of the teacher to support, empower, and help the student grow.

For many students, it can become quite difficult to follow along a path established by an adult, if the trust with that adult is highly compromised. Therefore, some students become interaction deprived. An interaction deprived student is a young person who is lacking the benefit of a reciprocal, genuine relationship. This can be exaggerated when such students encounter adults who have some of the characteristics of those whom they distrust. As a teacher, the types of interactions that you build with your students can impact the effectiveness of the culture for learning in and out of the classroom. The personalities of the adults and young people can clash but, with some variation in approach, those same interactions can be prosperous.

Imagine a student who enters your classroom each day appearing unmotivated, disconnected, and disengaged from the learning process. It may be easy to discount this student as unwilling to learn or uncaring. But imagine if you went to his/her home and realized that he/she, in fact, lives without basic necessities, such as food or proper clothing. This student may be forced to take on adult responsibility for which he/she has neither the maturity level nor skills to handle.

That knowledge about their history might affect how you interact with that student, meaning that one might be more understanding when addressing the student's needs, and the perception that he/she is unmotivated. It might even shine a light on the biases that one holds about other students because of their backgrounds and histories.

There are generally four identifiable pathways for most students. Those pathways are: driver, seeker, ranger, and the most difficult student to engage, armored. While these are the most common pathways, the authors believe that other pathways may emerge in the future. For example, one relationship management pathway the authors are currently researching is characterized by students with behaviors that desire more kinesthetic learning opportunities and the student who likes to entertain or be entertained by other disruptive students. Identifying which pathway to use with any given student is a critical part of implementing RMS™. Why?

Once the pathway is identified, the teacher can decide how to engage and empower these students using the most effective method and language— language that is authentic and genuine to their Personality Package™ and mantra. The Personality Package is an introspective self-analysis for adults developed by Parker Education & Development, LLC, to help identify the traits, characteristics, and dispositions to guide how they interact with others in a genuine manner. Ultimately, determining the pathway allows the teacher to make informed decisions based on evidence instead of relying on inferences and innuendos.

Young people express personality traits and mannerisms that they are exposed to on a regular basis. This might be exposure from parents, teachers, caregivers, friends, and so on. The exposure to their teacher's personality can lead to positive lifelong learning, or it might solidify the student's perceived notion of who the teacher really is, and how willing or unwilling that teacher is to make an impact in their lives. This chapter will not only define each pathway, but will a give specific description of the common characteristics of each, along with ineffective and effective approaches by our burgeoning staff members at Crummell Academy. The approach used to address the pathway may not be foolproof and it may require one to try various approaches until a positive relationship is solidified. Let us begin with the *driver* pathway.

## DRIVER STUDENTS

A student who is characterized as a driver typically seeks to control the classroom culture and climate. More than likely, this student has been placed in a position of control or adult responsibility at some point in his/her past school or familial experiences. Such students may have been disappointed by adults in their lives, or they have experienced limited to no support from the adults in their lives. This disappointment may, unfortunately, have come from a teacher. Therefore, in the classroom, the trust level is fragile. They seem to lead the class and do not appear to respect the position of the teacher as the authority figure in the classroom.

Drivers will generally:

- Deny relationships with most adults, especially the primary adult (teacher), with whom they spend the majority of their school related time.
- Create relationships with other adults to challenge the primary adult—teacher.
- Rally classmates to spearhead rebellion toward primary adult/teacher, if allowed.
- Do not always display a poor academic and negative behavioral outcomes.

### Making Connections: Drivers

This may be obvious, but drivers drive. They steer the classroom climate, and sometimes, their peers' behaviors. They attempt to build consensus with other students in an effort to challenge the teacher's authority. How, then, should one engage this type of student? Let's take a peek into Mr. Locklear's classroom and see how he manages the interactions with a driver student. This scenario illustrates one ineffective way of interacting with a driver.

*Bobby had a real knack for choosing the right time to challenge Mr. Locklear. His behavior usually led to at least half of the class criticizing Mr. Locklear's attempts at matching wits with Bobby. In the past, Bobby had found a way to capitalize on grammatical errors on the board or when Mr. Locklear did not have enough copies for all students.*

*This particular time, early December, while nearly everyone was desperately seeking a much needed winter break, Mr. Locklear wasn't in the most accepting and forgiving mood. Bobby proceeded to frankly explain to Mr. Locklear that yesterday's substitute teacher had taught them a different method of adding and subtracting fractions.*

*"Look! Bobby, you may think that you are on to something, but I guarantee you that what the sub showed you won't work always." As usual, Bobby led the charge for 50 percent of the students who wanted to use this different method. A very forceful and incendiary reply from Bobby included, "So you really don't care if we get the right answer or not...maybe we all should let our parents know you only want us to learn your way. . . . I think we should write the principal to let him know the sub was wrong." Mr. Locklear replied abruptly, "I'm the only one with the diploma and master's degree in here, people. I know what I'm doing so there's no need for the principal. Thank you very much."*

Mr. Locklear, perturbed by his student's dismissal of his instruction, decided to engage in a "bullfight" with Bobby in order to regain the steering wheel. In this context, a bullfight is when a male teacher attempts to engage in a game of one-upmanship with another male student. This is a highly ineffective approach that gives the power to the student and detracts from a healthy climate and a potentially positive relationship with the student. What would have been a more effective way for Mr. Locklear to handle this situation?

Mr. Locklear could have made his point to Bobby, as well as retained control of the class with a creative response. A response, such as, Mr. Locklear creating two problems, where the class uses the substitute's formula and Mr. Locklear uses the more accurate formula would allow the students options. It does not diminish the substitute's status and might possibly diminish Bobby's desire to drive the classroom and his peers' behavior. Bobby may retreat from the driver's seat realizing that he has more to learn. Mr. Locklear could have continued to use this as a teachable moment by focusing Bobby's attention on his own learning and behavior, thereby, maintaining a positive culture for learning to occur.

Certainly, this approach is not foolproof, but is an example of how one might address this type of behavior from a driver student. When working with driver students:

- Observe their behaviors, likes/dislikes to identify habits, especially when among friends and/or followers.
- Show patience, while strengthening their natural leadership skills.
- Respect their intelligence, however, the teacher must maintain his/her role as the authority figure within the classroom culture. Drivers need to know that while they think they have complete control of the car, the nearest adult is navigating with neutral conviction.

Let's now take a peek into Ms. Prentice's classroom to see how she interacts with a driver student. Ask yourself what you think about her approach, as you read through the scenario.

*Wynona was a very bright fourth grade student. She often found herself ahead of the class. Whenever this happened, without direction, she was quick to "assist" Ms. Prentice by giving other students the answers and not allowing them to complete their own work. Ms. Prentice had to constantly remind her to let teachers teach, and let students learn.*

*"But I'm just helping you out, Ms. Prentice. You know you need the help with these kids." Ms. Prentice replied, "You can't help me or anyone for that matter when you're a kid yourself. Just wait until you get a diploma." Wynona returned to her seat with a disgusted expression.*

## How Does This Scenario Represent an Ineffective Approach?

Ms. Prentice clearly is the leader of the class, but it's obvious that Wynona desires more challenging assignments. With this response, Ms. Prentice has negated a golden opportunity to enhance Wynona's learning. Without putting her too far ahead of the rest of the class, Ms. Prentice could have allowed Wynona to write some examples on the board, or prepare her ahead of time to assist other students properly, without just giving them answers. This would empower Wynona to drive herself, temporarily, and not engage in a "catfight" with the primary authority figure in the classroom. In this context, catfight is engaging in one-upmanship with a female teacher or authority figure.

## Think. Reflect. Connect.

Think of any students you have interacted with who were constantly attempting to "drive" the classroom culture. Use the questions below to think about how you might use this information to enhance your practices and approaches.

- At what point during the lesson were the driver students most disruptive or controlling?

- When interacting with a student with driver characteristics, how did you take into consideration their cognitive/intellectual ability?
- How did that affect your interactions with them in the future?

## SEEKER STUDENTS

There are students who suffer greatly from minimal to no interactions with adults. The interactions that they do experience are oftentimes forced or disingenuous. Therefore, these students may attempt to navigate a positive pathway toward growth of their character and dispositions without guidance from a more skilled and knowledgeable adult. This leads them to constantly seek attention. This attention seeking can result in negative or positive behaviors in order to monopolize the teacher's time, energy, and attention.

Seekers will:

- Sometimes be self-motivated to engage in activities and behaviors to avoid classwork.
- Be either A/B or D/F students. These students typically make really high or really low grades.
- Immediately try to gain exoneration from discipline, consequences, and so on, by pleasing the teacher.
- Bargain for the teacher's acceptance and/or attention.
- Have a personality that ranges from being a winner to a whiner.

Winners are defined as those students who might be the teacher's pet, or may come from perceived affluence that leads a teacher to trust that the home life might be stable, supportive, and loving home. This, in some cases, may be a veiled attempt by the family to create the perception of wholesomeness.

The whiners disengage before trying. They will divert the teacher's attention toward something irrelevant, such as, asking the teacher about their favorite TV show, or falsely claiming to be sick in order to retreat to the nurse's office. Certainly, there may be other characteristics, but these are few examples.

To create a more likely environment for more positive interactions, privileges, and incentives for behavior modification may work at a tier-three level. Not all students need incentives, so be wise and cautious about incentivizing good behavior. The goal is for students to place an intrinsic value on positive behavior, so much so that it becomes the desired choice. Be sure to avoid creating teacher's pet by not exempting them from any discipline with the rest of class. Offer only two paths—one similar to their choice and the other your desired choice. Elevate your desired choice as the nearest pathway to their own growth and independence, without the overwhelming attention of others. Do not succumb to their desired, attention-seeking choice.

## Making Connections: Seekers

In the following scenario, Mr. Locklear interacts with a seeker student. Let's take a peek into how he mishandled this pathway, followed by a more effective way in which he could have engaged with the seeker student.

*Cassandra was a new eighth grader to Crummell, who came to the school in October from a small border town in Texas. She was clearly enamored with Mr. Locklear. She made overt attempts to get him to notice her femininity. She was also an ELL—English Language Learner student who recently found out that she and Mr. Locklear shared similar Native American backgrounds. It was December and she did not have many friends. Cassandra desperately wanted to be accepted by her peers and by Mr. Locklear.*

*Cassandra frequently used her language barrier to work slowly, submit incomplete assignments, and become verbally disruptive with other students, knowing that Mr. Locklear would ultimately redirect her. She was seeking attention, avoiding work, and disrupting others. These are classic signs of a seeker student.*

*On this particular day, Cassandra attempted to entertain her peers at her table. A burst of laughter erupted from the back of the classroom. "Excuse me, table 3, I've had to address that table too many times today. Since you all can't stay focused on your lesson, I want you to get busy on your spelling words at your desk, please. You'll be making up this assignment during your recess. That includes you too, Cassandra!"*

*Cassandra responded slyly, "But I wasn't talking with them, Mr. Locklear. I was trying to listen to you, I promise, but I couldn't understand. Por favor, Mr. Locklear." Mr. Locklear initially resisted her attempt to gain exemption from the consequence, but eventually, after continued pleading on Cassandra's part, he succumbed. "You can wait at my desk until I'm finished here, Cassandra."*

Mr. Locklear can address Cassandra's need for academic attention and assistance without allowing her to monopolize his time or placate her girlish intentions. One approach could be to have her take ownership in helping herself first, before seeking adult attention. He can even have her keep a small running journal of how she has made attempts at helping herself first. Mr. Locklear should be able to manipulate the environment so that her future desire to seek extra attention is subdued. For Cassandra to believe in the proper pathway, she will need to absorb the small victories along the journey.

**Think. Reflect. Connect.**

Think of a student with whom you have interacted, who was constantly seeking attention from you, regardless of your responsibility to assist all students. Use the questions below to explore and reflect on how your approach helped or hindered the student's development and your effectiveness.

- What do you know about this student's background and motivation that might have facilitated his/her attention-seeking behaviors?
- How would you measure the effectiveness of the strategies that you might have used to interact with this student? What could you have done differently?
- How might you use what you now know about seeker students to enhance the strategy used?
- When interacting with this student, how did you take into consideration his/her cognitive/intellectual ability? How did that affect your interactions with the student?

## ARMORED STUDENTS

There are increasing numbers of young people who are unfortunately exposed to more than their fair share of adult experiences—experiences that far exceed their age and developmental stage—experiences that negatively shape their lives. These students are often polarized to life. These students may at times have experienced a number of heartbreaking moments and letdowns by the adults in their lives. At times, these students may have developed extreme negative views based on their experiences. They may even appear unmotivated to learn, uncaring, and unmoved by your attempt to connect with them.

Armored students will generally:

- Carry an emotional scar or burden that stems from their prior experiences and interactions with adults. They may harbor some deeply rooted emotional distress based on the hurtful words and actions of individuals they had presumed trustworthy.
- Show very little to no interest in any interactions with the teacher and/or other students.
- Sabotage the success of attempts by teachers or others to build positive relationships and any progress toward making those relationships meaningful.

In the school setting, many of these students develop a genuine distrust for adults, especially teachers who may have consciously or unconsciously marginalized their capabilities and abilities, and in some instances, their backgrounds. These students have similar characteristics of drivers, however, they don't seek control, but would rather hide and be forgotten. They are considered armored because over time these students have built a wall—a shield, to protect themselves emotionally. Let's revisit Mr. Locklear's classroom as he attempts to interact with an armored student. This scenario illustrates an ineffective approach to the armored student and pathway.

*Mr. Locklear was trying his best to relate to Josiyah. But, he couldn't seem to get this dejected young man to venture beyond his glaring exterior, an exterior that boasted a basketball height, a football frame, and the preconceived notion that he was too old for the eighth grade. Only Mr. Locklear knew that the awkward young man had a probation officer responsible for him every month. In contrast, it was well known by his peers that he was in and out of the foster care system because of his father's inability to take care of him. His mother died when he was just five years old. Moreover, his mobility fostered attendance issues, which ultimately affected his learning.*

*"It's good to see you, Josiyah. Welcome back to class! How was your Thanksgiving break?" "I didn't have a Thanksgiving," scoffed Josiyah, as he slid down into his seat. Mr. Locklear, to avoid the obvious and often obstinacy, quickly replied, "Well, you had to be thankful for something or someone. Even if it were to be out of school for three days. In fact, I don't remember seeing you that whole week before the holiday." With a menacing stare, Josiyah jabbed back by replying, "Ya know what, Mr. Lock-jaw," he said intentionally mispronouncing his name, "I was thankful for something. Missing this class for that long."*

*After some student oohs and aahs for that snappy comeback, most of the class settled down for instruction. Nevertheless, Josiyah still carried a bit of resentment for Mr. Locklear's comments and continued to disengage by rolling his eyes in disgust and laying his head down on the desk. He proceeded to periodically interfere with the lesson at hand with multiple attempts to see the nurse, visit the restroom, speak with the counselor, and so on. All of his attempts were met with negative responses, until Mr. Locklear obliged with a trip to the assistant principal's office with a referral for disrespect. "I hate this dude," Josiyah mumbled and smirked as he darted from the classroom and into the hallway presumably headed to Mrs. Franklin, the assistant principal's office.*

## What Might Have Been a More Effective Approach for Mr. Locklear to Implement?

A more effective approach to the armored student might include Mr. Locklear's deeper understanding of Josiyah's situation. With the knowledge that Mr. Locklear has about Josiyah's situation outside of school, he could have been more understanding of his attitude toward learning—an attitude that, most likely, has nothing to do with learning but more with his life circumstances. Creating a private moment, whether it be within the classroom or in the hall, would have put the two individuals at least on the pathway to better interactions. In addition, Mr. Locklear can express his expectations of Josiyah's behavior, along with the extension of emotional outreach for the larger than normal young man. Let us explore another example scenario.

In this next scenario, an ineffective approach to the armored student and pathway will be examined through an interaction in Ms. Prentice's classroom. Let's peek in on her classroom.

*"Come sit by me, Kendra. I'm saving your seat in this group," cried Maria. Maria made it no secret that she confided only in Kendra. Even though Kendra could only attend school about ten days per month due to her sickle-cell anemia condition, Maria truly looked forward to her presence. On this particular day, Kendra was only there for a short time in class. She received an early dismissal during the lesson at hand. This led to Maria suddenly retreating from participation.*

*Ms. Prentice had been attempting to make a connection with Maria since August. She was determined to bond with the distant nine-year-old by January. She understood Maria's struggles with being from a racially mixed background. Ms. Prentice even identified with her prepubescence physical development that clearly made Maria extremely uncomfortable and introverted. Ms. Prentice often discovered Maria in the hall crying or waiting to speak to Ms. Giovanni, one of the counselors. Aside from Kendra, she very rarely spoke to other students and avoided confiding in Ms. Prentice.*

*"Maria, I know you were looking forward to working with Kendra, but you can still get something accomplished. I'll even help you." "I don't feel good. Can I put my head down and just finish it for homework, Ms. Prentice?" Ms. Prentice carefully approached the introverted young girl and whispered to her, "Come on, Maria, I'll even let you turn in half the work for full credit. I understand how you feel. Please finish something to help your grade, Maria." Maria did not respond, kept her head on the desk, and completely disengaged from class. Ms. Prentice walked away in defeat, confirming the typical response Maria receives from adults.*

## How Might Ms. Prentice Been More Effective When Engaging with her Armored Student?

Ms. Prentice could foster a better interaction by sharing her own struggles during this difficult, unnerving time for a young female student. It is a risk, as Ms. Prentice cannot foresee how this information might be interpreted, however, students are asked to take a risk in trusting that that adult cares for, and not just about them. At times, it is important for students to see teachers as human, who might have experienced some of the same challenges. Affirming students' attempts to disengage from the learning process will only result in life continuing on the downward spiral.

Utilizing the obvious challenges that Maria is having with her outward appearance, Ms. Prentice can take small steps toward progress by privately discussing how she overcame her own issues. More importantly, she shouldn't openly press the issue of trying to build a relationship by pardoning her from academic expectations, having faith that when planting a seed of understanding and working to cultivate this seed, growth will be the result.

### Think. Reflect. Connect.

Think of a student or students you have tried to have interactions with, who distanced themselves from the rest of the class and other adults in the school. Think about and reflect on how you might have improved or enhanced your relatedness skills and techniques.

- What were the obvious or hidden extenuating circumstances, if any, which kept them from having meaningful interactions?
- How might you have your used your own experiences to create a bridge to connect with that student or students?
- If not through your experiences, in what ways or measures did you invest in some form of success for them?

To create a likely environment for more positive interactions, use patience, a mature wit and personal background knowledge to suggest or engage a productive approach to the pathway. The possibility of a relationship is based upon a firm understanding between the teacher and the student. Do not dwell upon minimal interaction, conversation, and/or compliance. Offer the opportunity to a successful pathway. The final pathway to explore in this chapter is the ranger. Ranger students are typically the students who require the teacher to modify and adjust the most because, at times, they may exhibit characteristics of many pathways.

## RANGER STUDENTS

Young people who are characterized as rangers generally show multiple signs and symptoms of interaction deprived students. They may begin showing signs, for example, of a driver, and then suddenly display a different set of characteristics throughout the remainder of the school year. There can be a myriad of reasons for this change. Rangers may be struggling with self-identity. They may be experiencing some devastating family challenges.

They may find a particular subject area difficult. They might be entering a phase where being accepted by peers is highly desired. Regardless of the reason, rangers can become difficult to interact with, because you are constantly adjusting your approach to the characteristics they display.

Rangers will:

- Usually be motivated extrinsically by the trends of their peers.
- Display multiple pathway characteristics, at times, due to traumatic events in their life.
- Believe that it's to their benefit to explore, or mimic other pathways, especially if they observe how other students manipulate the teacher and classroom climate and culture.
- Sometimes have difficulty finding their own genuine personality. They often borrow characteristics from their peers, especially characteristics that garner attention.

In the following scenario, Ms. Prentice is struggling with Justine, a student who exhibits multiple characteristics of various pathways.

*There was only one week of school left before the much anticipated winter break. Ms. Prentice normally counted on Justine following and supporting Carletta's misbehavior in class. Ms. Prentice's recognized that her frustration level increased when engaged with Seeker students. When working with Justine and Carletta, she redirected Justine more often than Carletta.*

*Ms. Prentice believed in Justine's ability to change her behavior and focus on her learning far more than Carletta, her counterpart. Strangely though, despite Carletta's instigating and leading, Justine had been quite withdrawn lately. Ms. Prentice was not aware that Justine's favorite grandmother was gravely ill and not expected to live through the holiday season. Nonetheless, she continued to redirect her, after Carletta became troublesome.*

*"Alright, Carletta, you are cruising for a detention young lady. And don't you even think about helping her disruptive behavior, Justine. I've had enough from the both of you that'll last me until we go on break." Carletta attempted to defend herself, "She didn't even see us talking, did she, Justine?" Justine looked down and said, "No," not really wanting to engage in a fight. Ms. Prentice paid no attention to the atypical response from Justine, issued both girls a detention slip and sent them to the assistant principal for further disciplinary action.*

**Based on What You Know about Ranger Students, How Might Ms. Prentice Have Handled This Situation Differently?**

Ms. Prentice could capitalize on her observing the initial change in Justine's behavior to inquire why the change may have occurred. In Justine's case, she is moving from being a driver, to being an armored student. With the knowledge that she has obtained through her observations, Ms. Prentice could manipulate the environment that addresses the characteristics of an armored student by opening the possibility of some positive interactions with Justine and acknowledging the behavior she used to display with Carletta. In a private moment, Ms. Prentice could have initiated some dialog with Justine, which might have allowed her to discuss any issues without her peers' knowledge. This would have helped Justine see Ms. Prentice as not just her teacher, but an adult whom she can trust, and perhaps, confide in.

**Think. Reflect. Connect.**

Think of a student or students you've tried to have interactions with who showed distinct characteristics of one pathway, and later on in the school year began exhibiting characteristics of another pathway.

- What were the apparent behavioral changes that made you recognize that there was a change happening with this student or students?
- Young people experiment with various characteristics, some are authentic to their personality, and others are learned traits and dispositions. Based on what you now know about ranger students, when, and how soon should adults change their strategies and approaches to better support those students' learning, and why?
- When interacting with a student who's displaying multiple characteristics, what would account for the impact that his/her behavior might have on his/her behavior and learning?

## OTHER CONSIDERATIONS AND FINAL THOUGHTS

It can become complex to keep track of the many characteristics and personalities you will encounter within just one classroom culture. It is important to note that not all students will be interaction deprived. In fact, you will find a large percentage of students adhering to the classroom procedures, expectations, and routines set forth. However, those students who are interaction deprived can change the character and climate dramatically. These distractions can lead to a disruptive learning environment.

If a firm and consistent structure is implemented and supported, then those students needing extra or more intensive intervention will reveal themselves in due time, at which point a pathway approach can be applied without totally dismantling the learning environment. To create a likely environment for more positive interactions, show patience with fluctuations in behaviors and difficult ordeals.

Also, explore why the fluctuations in behavior are occurring. This allows you to guide the student behavior and actions that will be most supportive to their learning. When applicable, utilize other pathway guidelines to effectively support students' desire to grow, learn, and live authentically.

Some additional and relevant guidelines to further confirm the language, tone, and approaches include:

- Seekers will seek attention, negative or positive, from students and/or adults. Offer positive attention whenever earned. Refrain from giving the student(s) constant negative attention and language. This will surely weaken the relationship.
- Drivers are clever at selecting your weakest or most unorganized moment in an attempt to drive the classroom culture. Make every attempt to stay two steps ahead of them, yet recognize and forgive yourself if you cannot maintain that level of fortitude.
- Rangers, over time, will display different characteristics. Don't confuse a change in mood, season, or building climate with a fluctuation in personality. For example, a student who was cut from the cheerleading team might just need time to grieve over his/her loss.
- Armored students may take the longest amount of time before you experience or observe a breakthrough, but they require a more careful, sensitive form of interaction. Sometimes your presence is more impactful than your words.
- Be willing to follow the advice of other adults who have had successful interactions with the same students with whom you have unsuccessfully interacted with.

In chapter 7, the reader will be introduced to a set of techniques designed to engage students who need more intensive intervention to avoid a potentially unsafe situation. The D.E.P.T.H. Anchor Strategy can be a valuable tool to protect persons, personhood, and property. It is a go-to strategy to address highly contentious, emotional situations. It is the hope of the authors that this be the least used strategy, but it is valuable when needed in order to maintain order and safekeeping.

*Chapter 7*

# D.E.P.T.H. Anchor Strategy

*Don't fear the consequence of reachable expectations.*

*T. Parker*

So far, this section of the book has offered a classroom routine strategy—Monitor 2 Modify (M2M), and routes to potentially positive relationships with interaction deprived students—Relationship Management Pathways (RMPs).

As seen in figure 7.1, this chapter introduces D.E.P.T.H. Anchor, a strategy reserved for diffusing disruptive, cantankerous, and potentially dangerous situations.

Figure 7.1   RMSTM – D.E.P.T.H. Anchor.

The purpose of the D.E.P.T.H. Anchor Strategy is to ensure that the classroom and school environment are grounded, hooked, or "anchored" to a sense of emotional and physical safety for all. This strategy greatly supports the Interaction Congruence Theory (ICT) components of responsiveness, rapport, and respect because it is designed to attend to social-emotional learning, safety, adult-to-student, and student-to-student interactions.

D.E.P.T.H. Anchor is a teacher-initiated strategy that includes five techniques to help the user remember the steps and actions to engage when faced with emotionally charged, volatile situations. The authors recommend this strategy be reserved for the more chaotic situations and events (e.g., fights, highly emotional arguments, threats to other students' person/personhood and/or property, or damage to school property). While this strategy may be used to defuse volatile situations, using the techniques may also create opportunities for social and emotional learning.

Each technique allows one to impact an individual student or a group of students' behaviors, emotionality, actions, and dispositions to deescalate an event or activity. In those moments, or even at a later time, the teacher might engage in a teachable moment to regain or maintain a calm, caring, and civil climate. For example, when engaging the *Emotion* technique, it will be important to take measure of one's emotional temperature before reacting to a situation.

Figure 7.2 depicts the D.E.P.T.H. Anchor chart descriptors. The techniques in the strategy are not necessarily designed to be used in sequence. For example, one may need to engage the specific technique that is necessary for the event or occurrence. Dealing with the *Emotion* technique may be important before utilizing the *Dispersing* technique. Other situations might require a call for immediate assistance first, the *Help* technique. The figure below shows both the teacher-initiated strategies and the social and emotional opportunities students may embrace and learn.

The national, local news, and various social media outlets are not in short supply of stories where students and educators are faced with active shooter situations, out of control parents, unethical, and sometimes volatile teachers, and students engaging in gross disrespect of staff. While outside events are not always controllable, dangerous situations incited by those from within the school culture can be, and must be, curbed. Proper implementation of the D.E.P.T.H. Anchor Strategy from all staff members can assist greatly in anchoring any school climate, like that of a ship in a storm.

As with previous chapters, Crummell will be revisited, allowing the reader a peek into Mr. Locklear and Ms. Prentice's classrooms. Mr. Locklear and Ms. Prentice have been working in collaboration for several months to implement the Relationship Management System (RMS)™ system. Both have experienced positive changes. Yet, Ms. Prentice continues to struggle in a few areas, mainly when it comes to students exhibiting a lack of self-control and

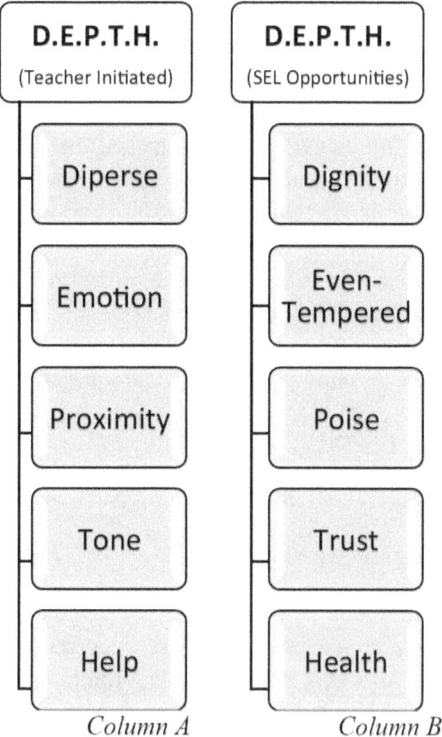

Figure 7.2  D.E.P.T.H Anchor Strategy.

allowing their emotionality to manifest as angry verbal outbursts, and in some instances, physical violence.

*Over the past several weeks, Mr. Locklear and Ms. Prentice both experienced some success in implementing M2M. Ms. Prentice, especially found that her students were more responsive in class and engaged in far fewer negative behaviors. She used the information on RMPs that Mr. Locklear shared to identify who many of her students were. Surprisingly, many of her students were armored, although she had a few key students who were drivers. Once she acknowledged the path—the specific route those students used to interact, gain attention and connect—she modified her behavioral interventions to meet the needs of each student.*

*She was proud of the changes she had seen so far. Still, Ms. Prentice was having great difficulty when students' negative behaviors increased or situations erupted in the classroom. She had to use the safety officer far more than other teachers in her grade, or even in the building, to break up fights and squelch potentially dangerous situations. Just a few weeks ago, Ms. Prentice had to break up a fight between two rival girls.*

*Even though her classroom management was better, Ms. Prentice was still considered a pushover by the students. Plus, she had started to receive complaints from parents about their child's learning. She began preparing for parent-teacher conferences and relied on a strategy she had used for the past two years—P.R.P.L.E. Sandwich.* This strategy will be detailed in chapter 8.

*For now, her goal was to find some way to be more effective when dealing with situations that needed a more intense intervention. She remembered Mr. Locklear shared an acronym, D.E.P.T.H., with her, which she thought might help. She decided to find him after school to revisit what it meant and how to use it. After school Ms. Prentice and Mr. Locklear met in her room to discuss D.E.P.T.H. Anchor.* The next few sections will define and discuss this strategy in more detail and how to use the technique effectively.

## D.E.P.T.H. ANCHOR STRATEGY

### Disperse Technique

There may be times in which young people will partake in behaviors deemed as turbulent and incendiary. Hopefully, these occurrences are minimal. Yet, the first technique of the **D**.E.P.T.H. strategy refers to dispersing students before they have the chance to become participants or incite bystanders to join an altercation. Bystanders are those members of the immediate environment who can potentially get involved by verbally or physically encouraging the respective participants to continue engaging in inappropriate, potentially dangerous behavior.

### Using the Disperse Technique Effectively

There are several considerations for using the *Disperse* technique effectively. There are identified below.

- The most important step in using this technique effectively is to first determine that the situation can be controlled, while attempting to disperse students. For example, if there are numerous student bystanders gathered around a highly emotional and contested situation, you might need to engage the *Help* technique. It is first and foremost the responsibility of school personnel to ensure that students are physically and emotionally safe.
- If it is deemed that you can control the environment, give the nonparticipating students a verbal directive to move away from the area. This may lessen the cosigning by the crowd or key instigators.

- Physically escort students safely to another area, when in danger, to prevent any casualties. However, remember that you have to assess the situation to ensure that you alone can manage and disperse students, when necessary. Certainly, whenever physically moving students, you want to follow your district and school policies.

In all fairness, most young people do not desire to participate in raucous behaviors. It is quite the contrary. However, if the teacher has loose, limited, or is lacking classroom policies, procedures, expectations and routines, an environment conducive to multiple outbursts can be created. In these instances, even those who might typically disengage from raucous behavior could be more inclined to engage inappropriately. Sometimes peer pressure, bullying, and instigation by their peer group may play a huge role in bystander participation. But again, using this technique goes deeper than reacting to an event. There may also be a social-emotional learning opportunity.

When applying the "D"—*Disperse*—technique, one may also have the opportunity to teach students **Dignity—a sense of worth, value, self-respect, pride**. For example, removing the audience—the bystanders, can aid in defusing the emotionality connected to what may have started as verbal banter. This allows those involved to retain or regain a positive student status, which is important to most students. It also fosters a sense of certainty for the bystanders that their behavior is also deemed inappropriate and will not be tolerated or excused. The next technique, *Emotion*, is critical and essential to utilize at all times.

The *Emotion* technique allows one to take a self-inventory to avoid any appearance of favoritism and punitive action because of the adrenaline, or past experiences with a student, or the emotional response that may rise up based on one's own history.

## Emotion Technique

The next technique in D.E.P.T.H. Anchor is *Emotion*. Emotions may run really high, very quickly, in certain situations while working with young people. As an adult, it is imperative to remain calm yourself, while also respecting the potential for the student's emotions to rise. This technique is a reminder to control or monitor one's emotions to make informed, balanced decisions. It is well understood that when emotion rises, intellect decreases. Therefore, as the teacher, you want to gather your emotions so as not to make rash decisions based on past events, history, or experiences with any particular student that could spark an emotional response.

## Using the Emotion Technique Effectively

As with the *Disperse* technique, there are several aspects to effective implementation of the *Emotion* technique. These are listed below.

- Take deep breaths to find calm and centeredness.
- The *Emotion* technique can be mastered by practicing monitoring your emotional level under conditions where the emotionality of a situation might be less for an adult. An example of this is counseling a distraught student, who is upset because their friend wrote an undesirable post on a popular social media site.
- When multiple students express heightened emotions, the environment may be subdued by the teacher maintaining a low emotional level or an even emotional level. Practicing this technique will only make it easier to counter an emotionally charged situation where demonstrating level-headedness is necessary.
- Decide on how to intervene when the student or students' emotions are high. Avoid the emotionality that can lead to the student or the teacher making poor decisions. Having an audience of bystanders nearby can potentially make the immediate climate of the situation more difficult for students or teachers to make a wise decision. Therefore, reducing the emotion and removing the factors that might add fuel to the emotional situation so that other students are not negatively influenced is just as critical.
- There are some who might discount the human emotional factor in young people. Yet, young people carry emotions that can be real and raw, at times, to the dismay of adults. Their world, experiences, and trials may seem trivial to adults, but for young people, they may be huge and all encompassing. A friend who ended a friendship to join a new friendship circle can be devastating for a young person.
- Exercise some empathy with the students and remember that as an adult you may have had similar experiences that challenged your younger years. Sharing those similar experiences in a timely manner not only helps build a bond with the young person, but it also humanizes the adult. Remember that you too were once their age.
- Challenge the situation with calm, collectedness, certainty, and composure.
- Consider the age appropriateness of the student and how the student might be emotionally affected by the situation, even if you believe it to be insignificant. The adult should model the appearance of balanced temperament. For example, if a student is displaying uncontrollable emotions, it would be wise for the adults to control their own physical and verbal responses, such as refraining from body language that shows frustration or using patronizing language. So goes the phrase, "Practice makes perfect!"

Use the *Emotion* technique early and often. When using this technique with fidelity and consistency, the teacher models **Even Temperedness—stable, composed, level-headedness** for his/her student body. Students will observe your effective modeling of how you controlled your behavior, actions, and attitudes to reach a positive outcome. The next technique in the strategy is *Proximity* which addresses how one uses body positioning to maintain the positive classroom environment and manage student behaviors.

## Proximity Technique

Proximity is very important in the process of monitoring the climate of the classroom or building. It is the next technique in D.E.**P**.T.H. Many times, just the presence of an adult or teacher will curb any problematic occurrences. It is well documented that proximity can be useful and valuable to classroom management. However, there must be a balance between using proximity and the reinforcement of classroom expectations and procedures in a controlled environment, as the authors discussed in chapter 5—"Monitor 2 Modify (M2M)."

## Using the Proximity Technique Effectively

Careful attention to the elements of the Proximity technique will ensure successful implementation. These components are identified below.

- When using this technique, the teacher should always maintain quality vantage points. Vantage points are positions within the classroom environment in which the adult is able to maintain a quality view of all students. Young people will periodically challenge this technique with diversions. These can include taking advantage of the teacher's focus on students in a guided reading group by participating in horseplay, or intentionally blocking a teacher's vantage point for others to engage in mischief. With practice, teachers can adjust their proximity control based on the physical space and anticipate student behaviors, so these potential diversions are alleviated.
- Continuously utilize the physical space to position oneself to control or guide students' attention, behavior, and actions. Setting this expectation creates an environment where students are aware that the teacher will redirect, stand close to, and reinforce expectations when needed. This can be used inside the classroom, in the hallway, or wherever students might need some directions and support in focusing their attention.
- Do not hover over students, or stand by the same student or group of students for prolonged periods of time. This might give the appearance of unfairness.

*Proximity* is a widely used technique to support the classroom environment. Like all other techniques, it is most effective when used on a consistent basis. The relationship between teacher and students will blossom as they witness the regular habit of the teacher being prepared to protect the learning environment. Students will feel secure as the teacher moves about the room and uses *Proximity* as a consistent technique. This technique may effectively ensure students that you are near and are aware they need redirection or that they need to refocus their attention.

As a caveat, it has been the experience of one of the authors, as a male educator, that most male students, especially, will give ample notice of a potential altercation. This notice will result in heightened sounds and voices. It might be boastful language loud enough for a teacher to hear. It might be an inflection in the voice or tone that draws attention. It could be a chorus of noises and sounds from a growing group of bystanders. All of which are cries for adult intervention. Why?

For many young male students, there is a tendency to inflate emotional responses and vibrato to impress and give the appearance of hyper masculinity. Peer pressure can sometimes play a huge role in the decisions young males make—decisions that are not always well informed. Brain research provides some explanation into why this type of response occurs.

The amygdala is a part of brain that continues to grow during the young adult years. It is responsible for emotional responses, survival, and memory. Because this part of the brain is continuing to develop, young males, influenced in many ways by society's perception of masculinity, may not yet understand how to avoid or discard insults to pride and person. This may lead to poor decisions and risky behavior, especially in group situations.

For example, two male students begin a verbal disagreement in the hallway. Once enough peers begin to gather around the two males to form an audience, you may find the two male participants raising their voices or flaunting their masculinity with threatening words and gestures. At this juncture, neither of the male students is in a position to retreat, particularly if there is mounting pressure from the peer group surrounding them. Nevertheless, they anticipate and desire an adult to intervene on their behalf.

The adult intervention allows the two males to avoid any physical confrontation or the fear of being ridiculed by their peers. This avoidance of confrontation can be addressed by the adult using proper proximity control. While this caveat is specific to male students, there is an emergence of girls engaging in similar behaviors. The authors, in fact, assert that the *Proximity* technique is helpful to manage the classroom and student behaviors effectively regardless of the students' gender.

As mentioned earlier in this chapter, most students do not want to engage in altercations and cantankerous situations. It is quite the opposite. Most students are struggling to find a place of belonging. They want to be accepted by their peers and peer groups, and their teachers. So, as the author/s have experiences, often times, when a male student, in particular, increases his volume, it is with the hope that an adult will prevent the potentially dangerous situation from escalating. Proper proximity, free of haphazard approaches from the teacher, can also set a positive precedent for the other techniques within this strategy.

When proper proximity is used, the teacher is in effect modeling **Poise—demonstrating balance, elegance, and grace** for the students. For the male student, from the male author's perspective, it is important for the educator to model poise so they, the male students, learn:

- It is not always necessary to display hyper masculinity when involved in high emotional situations. By simply staying balanced within oneself, male students can view someone demonstrating control.
- Poise can increase a young male's skill for exhibiting grace under pressure, balance, and how to assess a potentially unsafe situation. By remaining poised, that male student can exercise his knowledge and retreat to, or move to, a safer place to avoid continued threats of person and/or property.

In general, all students, male and female, observe how the teacher is creating a balanced, controlled classroom climate. The teacher may model and coach students to demonstrate poise, balance, and grace. They begin to understand that in this kind of classroom, learning is the expectation. Misbehavior is addressed effectively, or is suspended, or eradicated, and students feel physically and emotionally secure. Following the *Proximity* technique is arguably one of the more commonly misconstrued techniques, **Tone**.

## Tone Technique

This technique can be easily misconstrued with volume, or raising one's voice while using stern language. In contrast, using the *Tone—D.E.P.T.H.*—technique means to apply firm, even, concise language to gather control of a situation. *Tone* can be characterized as using your credible voice and not your invitational voice.

With a credible voice, there is no inflection of a question at the end of your statement or response. Typically, your voice lowers half an octave to a full octave. When using an invitational voice, there is usually an inflection of a question at the end of the statement or response. The tone is at a higher octave than one's normal speaking voice.

## Using the Tone Technique Effectively

Successful implementation of the *Tone* technique will be enhanced by attending to these recommendations.

- Establish the tone at the beginning of the relationship, without attaching negative connotations or consequences. A firm tone can and will be respected by the student body.
- Utilizing the student's name, if applicable, stating the consequences, and/or giving physical redirection while using a credible tone, can be beneficial in defusing a potentially negative situation. A sense of seriousness and control will be established.
- As with the M2M strategy, you want to establish a sense of control without being controlling. In this context, however, it might be that as the adult in the classroom, you implement this technique to solidify yourself as accountable for the culture of learning created in that classroom. In essence, *Tone* is deeper than one's actual tone of voice. *Tone* can also support a positive classroom environment. Setting the tone—the climate—early in the school year can be more beneficial in defusing unwanted events later and throughout the remainder of the school year. Therefore the teacher should use a combination of voice tone and setting a class tone to anchor the technique in the environment.
- Regardless of the credibility of the tone, a teacher should avoid overusing a firm voice tone only when students are misbehaving so that its effect will not be diminished as the school year progresses. For example, if a student is misbehaving, one might use a credible tone to redirect, just as one might use a credible tone when a student is engaged and focused on his/her work.

The perception of some skeptics is that young people will respond negatively to a firm tone. It may be perceived as harsh or unforgiving. Not so. A firm tone may *command* attention much like a leader who demonstrates how to complete a task, instead of just demanding the staff to complete a task with little to no guidance. In the classroom, students, then, can correct their behavior based on your demonstration of appropriate behaviors and actions. A commanding tone is especially useful if the credible tone is not overused.

Appropriate use of *Tone* allows the social-emotional opportunity for students to take away a sense of **Trust** that the adult will be fair, reliable, honorable, convicted, and principled. Otherwise, poor attempts at using tone throughout the year can demand attention temporarily, but that attention will eventually wane. This technique, like all others, requires practice so that teachers will not resort to yelling or using redundant language.

A distinction in various tones can range from using definitive verbiage versus inquisitive verbiage. An example of using definitive verbiage might be, "We **WILL** learn our line-up procedure in class, even if it takes the entire period. Or, another example could be "Ridiculing others **WILL NOT** be tolerated in this class! Am I understood?" Both are effective and support students' understanding of the classroom rules and expectations. Inquisitive verbiage might be, "Why are we not lining up properly, class?" or "Should I be taking recess from you guys? Is that what you guys want?" This type of language allows more wiggle room within the routine than needed and will quickly diminish the climate and culture.

The last, and some may believe the most misused, technique is the *Help* technique. Much like *Disperse*, it is important to first assess when to request help.

## Help Technique

The final technique in D.E.P.T.H is *Help*. This technique keeps students safe, as well as averts the escalation of an incident. It is the act or action of requesting assistance after assessing what type of support is needed. When using this technique properly, a teacher can also strengthen the relationship between colleagues and parents. It is important that the teacher does not abuse this resource. For example, it would not be wise to request rapid help to halt bickering between 1st graders. Concurrently, a female high school teacher who is witnessing two male students in the hall engaging in fisticuffs should immediately request assistance. Why?

Physically intervening between two young adult male students may cause bodily harm to a female teacher. Likewise, a male middle school teacher diffusing a situation between two female students may request help from a female teacher to avoid a potentially uncomfortable situation and/or unwarranted allegations from the female students.

## Using the Help Technique Effectively

Below are several ideas to assist in the successful implementation of the *Help* technique.

- When getting help from another adult to diffuse a situation, a teacher should take into account the age, gender, and size of the student or students involved.
- A teacher can ask for help from an administrator, counselor, or even a parent. Of course, if the situation calls for immediate assistance, there should be a protocol available to request assistance.

- If the need for assistance is not imminent, the adult can be flexible in measuring the type of help necessary for the incident. For example, if a student engages in an inappropriate action that is not necessarily dangerous, help might come in the form of parental involvement. This can be especially true when the teacher has developed a healthy relationship with the parent or parents, and all parties are of one accord in terms of the student's behavior and actions. To continue with the example, help might also come from an internal resource or other types of external resources, like a school counselor, behavioral interventionist, or mental health provider.

For the sake of the climate, and ultimately the culture of learning, the social-emotional opportunity for all stakeholders is **Health.** This will ensure that students feel emotionally secure and safe, and the mental wellness of all is fostered. Let's see how Mr. Locklear and Ms. Prentice use the D.E.P.T.H. Anchor Strategy and techniques to interaction with their students.

*Mr. Locklear and Ms. Prentice collapsed in the only two adult chairs in Ms. Prentice's classroom. They had made it through another school day only a couple of weeks after the winter break. Very few people had made the adjustment to being back in school, and it showed on Ms. Prentice and in her classroom. Mr. Locklear shared a success story about using D.E.P.T.H. Anchor in his classroom. Ms. Prentice was very interested at this point, considering that she was at a loss for maintaining any positive interactions.*

*"You have to understand that young people need to know you'll keep them safe while in your presence. And I've realized that isn't always about physical safety, but emotional as well. Peer pressure is at an all-time high these days, Ms. Prentice. Just the other day, I had two 8th graders in class starting to jaw at each other over. . . . I can't even remember what it was about. Anyway, I could tell it was about to escalate, even after I told them to cool it. I could actually feel myself getting angry at them not listening to me. I was already in the worst mood and these guys were starting up during first period!"*

*Ms. Prentice listened a bit more closely because she found herself in situations like this often, especially as she felt herself becoming more and more upset at the students' defiance. Mr. Locklear continued, "Strangely, I thought of the D.E.P.T.H. Anchor Strategy from the workshop. I gathered my emotions first before I said anything else. Just a couple of deep breaths while these two guys rose from their seats. I could see some other students egging them on, and I immediately put a stop to them by promising any bystanders that they would incur detentions, even if they said one word."*

*"By this time, I had slowly approached the guys while they were waiting for the other to buckle first. That was using proximity, as well as when I stepped between them and directed Jeffrey to step outside. He froze and didn't look like he was calming down. I then used a firmer tone and simply said, 'Jeffrey.*

Outside. Now.' He began to comply and eventually made it to the hall. I was surprised that it worked the way it was supposed to. I could see that Jeffrey was still pretty upset, even fighting back tears. It was nearing the end of the period, and I saw Ms. Giovanni walking towards us. I asked if she could take him to her office for a while. That was like getting help from the D.E.P.T.H. Anchor Strategy."

Ms. Prentice looked somewhat relieved that her colleague was able to apply some of the strategies from the Relationship Management workshop. She hoped that Mr. Locklear could share more experiences like these with her to boost her confidence. She was beginning to feel a bit rundown from all the necessary implementations. Mr. Locklear exited Ms. Prentice's room, but not without displaying an expression of determination for her benefit. She absorbed his encouraging expression and decided to leave herself. While walking to her car, she could faintly hear her name being called. It sounded like an adult's voice, in distress, coming from the quad area.

"Ms. Prentice, Ms. Prentice, please help me! I need you!" It was the assistant principal, Mrs. Franklin, trying to prevent a fight between a group of guys and one Crummell student. Ms. Prentice saw one of the guys from the group was a former student of hers and was now in the ninth grade. Ms. Prentice quickly made her way over to where Ms. Franklin stood appearing nervous and frantic. "What's going on over here?" Ms. Prentice demanded. Mrs. Franklin replied, "These 9th graders won't stop harassing Samuel. I've told them to leave the premises too, many times. Can you call the resource officer, please?"

Suddenly, something came over Ms. Prentice. She quickly gathered her emotions and addressed the young man whom she had as a student previously. "Nicholas, what are you doing with these guys, harassing Samuel?" she questioned with a firm tone. "Mrs. Franklin told you guys to leave and I'd advise you all to do so, now." She could see that, similar to Mrs. Franklin's request, it was falling on defiant ears. Samuel was on guard and preparing himself for a physical ambush from the bunch.

Ms. Prentice realized that while the young men were in a fighting stance, neither of them was making a concerted effort to engage in a fight. At this point, Ms. Prentice positioned herself partly in front of Samuel, but not so much as to be physically harmed should the situation escalate. She utilized her proximity wisely, though, by not taking her eyes off the group and raising her open hand to them, peaceably.

"Get outta the way, Ms. Prentice," said Nicholas, with a panicked voice. She rebutted even firmer and with a more credible tone than before, "Nicholas! I said leave. Right now!" While Ms. Prentice intervened, Mrs. Franklin managed to reach the resource officer on her cellphone. He rushed from outside the building and over to the quad only to see the group of guys running *away from the situation. He escorted the shaken Samuel inside the building to call home. Mrs. Franklin abruptly thanked Ms. Prentice for her assistance. "I'm so glad you were able to step in when you did, Ms. Prentice, and I speak for Samuel as well, I'm sure." Ms. Prentice took some more deep breaths before entering her car and driving home.*

Many teachers dread this type of scenario ever happening in their presence. Yet, situations like this may occur when supervising young people. Even after Assistant Principal Franklin requested Ms. Prentice to bring the resource officer, she took it upon herself to verbally and physically intervene. Her confidence came from recognizing one of the young men, which may not always be the case. Therefore, use discretion and caution when deciding to expose yourself to bodily harm. Again, depending upon the relationship of the parties involved, factors for consideration by a teacher before stepping in to physically intervene include:

- One's own physical health,
- The physical stature and weight of the parties involved,
- The likelihood of the situation escalating without some type of physical intervention,
- Prior training in crisis intervention methodologies, and
- Students' individual behavior intervention plans.

The authors, again, caution and recommend that teachers should always follow their district and school policies when physically intervening with students.

**Think. Reflect. Connect.**

Think of a time in which you, or a colleague, were involved in a situation that could have potentially escalated quickly into a volatile or dangerous situation. Think about, reflect upon, and make connections to the ways in which this information may enhance your current strategies and techniques.

- How did your emotions, during the situation, affect your thinking process?
- How could you have used the D.E.P.T.H. Anchor Strategy, explicitly, to foster a safe and secure environment for those involved in that situation?
- If there were any bystanders, how did they impact the participants involved?
- Why do you think proximity is so important in maintaining the sanctity of the environment?

This strategy is a collection of techniques designed to readily address situations within the classroom, building, or on campus premises that have the potential to move quickly to an unsafe and undesirable state. The strategy is meant to maintain the relationship between all parties involved while de-escalating any potential hazardous behaviors.

## FINAL THOUGHTS

As a visual/mental cue for this strategy, remember D.E.P.T.H. describes both teacher-initiated and social-emotional opportunities:

- **Disperse** to maintain **Dignity**.
- **Emotional** check maintains an **Even temperament**.
- **Proximity** check with caution to maintain **Poise**.
- **Tone** in voice, not volume, will display **Trust**.
- **Help**, when applicable, will maintain **Health**.

In the next chapter, the authors will present a communication and feedback strategy—P.R.P.L.E. Sandwich. While it has a funny name, this strategy is a collection of techniques developed to provide constructive feedback and support in order to foster, motivate, and support students' finding success. Chapter 8 will also revisit Ms. Prentice and Mr. Locklear as they continue to implement the RMS™ strategies.

*Chapter 8*

# P.R.P.L.E. Sandwich Strategy

*Creating a bridge between the ideal and the real.*

C. Barnes

As seen in figure 8.1, this chapter will explain the P.R.P.L.E Sandwich, our final strategy, for this book, in the Relationship Management System (RMS)™. This is a communication and feedback strategy, which addresses the intentionality in which we create opportunities for mutual trust and respect to develop. It also addresses the art of managing strategy that addresses the art of managing a relationship within the education environment. It is a series of prompts that, when layered effectively, speak to how two or more people can express concerns without the adverse feeling of not being fully heard or respected.

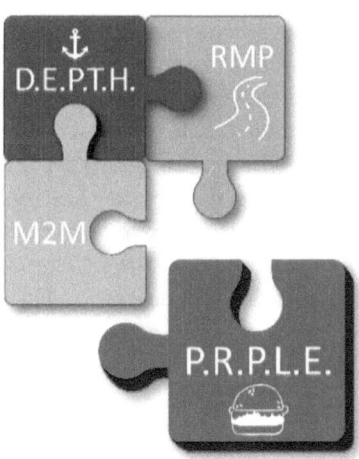

Figure 8.1 RMSTM – P.R.P.L.E. Sandwich.

The strategy can be used in all facets of the educator's realm, including communication with students, parents, and even colleagues. One advantage of using this strategy is that it can be utilized by anyone who struggles with confrontational situations. Thus, those who tend to exit conversations prematurely, to avoid the inevitable conflict, can rest easier that the other party or parties can make solid decisions. We invite the reader to experience how Mr. Juarez, school counselor, and Ms. Prentice explore the use of the P.R.P.L.E. Sandwich Strategy in preparation for parent conferences.

*Ms. Prentice has used the communication and feedback strategy— P.R.P.L.E. Sandwich, for the past two months. It was evident that, here in early March, this was her strongest and most consistent strategy. Even though her classroom management was a challenge, she could always rely on using this strategy to impact the relationships that she had with the families under her care. It was the one area where she scored "outstanding" on her teacher performance evaluation.*

*Coincidentally, one of the school counselors, Mr. Juarez, was introduced to the strategy in the RMS™ professional development he attended. He was anxious to implement the strategy during the next parent-teacher conference night. Typically, he experienced low attendance at parent-teacher conference night. Often times, the families he worked with received such negative commentary from teachers that they had become accustomed to negative comments. Even though he was the counselor, they expected the same from Mr. Juarez. Why would they expect anything different?*

*This time he hoped for a better turnout. For the past several weeks, Mr. Juarez had made sure to send promising and positive comments and reports home. Sometimes he called the families. Other times he sent an email. Occasionally, he sent out a group text message to his group of parents, proclaiming the day to be overwhelmingly productive. His hope was that parents would take a chance and come to parent-teacher conference night, with the hopes of hearing more positive and encouraging news about their child's progress.*

*Mr. Juarez certainly wanted to share positive thoughts, but there were also some challenges that needed to be discussed. Still, he also wanted to make sure that the families knew their child's potential. He wanted to find a way to leverage the positive for increased productivity and progress, so that students would feel empowered. He knew using the P.R.P.L.E. Sandwich Strategy would be effective. However, he needed help in organizing how to share this information appropriately, and he needed practice in articulating his thoughts in an authentic way.*

*Ms. Prentice, having used this strategy more than a few times, was happy to coach Mr. Juarez through organizing his thoughts, data, student's work, and so on, to effectively share the information with families. After all, Mr. Juarez had been incredibly helpful to her over the past several months. Later* in the week, Ms. Prentice and Mr. Juarez sat down to discuss how she used the strategy effectively, and how Mr. Juarez might consider using the strategy to support and empower his students. They also spent some time practicing what he wanted to say to parents so that it sounded authentic, conversational, and not robotic or forced.

When it comes to communication, many people believe that open and honest is the best policy. Supposedly, this will ensure that all parties involved can exit the conversation satisfied. However, when it comes to thorough, concise communication to maintain a productive relationship, layering a conversation properly tends to be the most productive policy. This layering, much like a sandwich, can be accomplished with moderate practice. It also fosters more constructive feedback and allows all the parties involved to exit the conversation well informed. Goals can be set with measurable benchmarks and roles can be clearly defined.

## P_ositive

There's nothing more effective than being positive when beginning a conversation. Lead the conversation with something affirming, preferably with some evidence known to both parties. A current occurrence is usually most helpful to stabilize the conversation. This will ease the tension of delicate situations. In this early part of the conversation, one should lead with "I Feel" statements. Creating a practice of beginning with something positive will build a rapport with others that will benefit future interactions. Some examples include: "I Feel you're at your best when . . . " or "I Feel you've got major upside in this area . . . " or "I Feel you have what it takes to. . . . " When attempting to communicate thoroughly, keep "I Feel" statements focused on the positive.

Subsequently, be sure the "I Feel" statements are kept to a minimum and only with expressing something positive. Beginning the conversation with positive comments sets a tone that invites participants to fully engage. As educators, there are many instances when comments are deficit focused, and this negative tone can be detrimental to communication. To safeguard against the conversation losing its focus, be sure to take into account the perspectives of the other members of the conversation. Whether the conversation is with another teacher, a student, or a parent, it may help guide their feedback by asking, "How do you feel about . . . ?" or "What are your feelings about . . . ?"

## R_eality

After a positive introduction to a conversation, the reality of the situation can be expressed. In fact, if performed properly, this prompt allows for confidence in delivering concrete information. Even though the delivery of information may cause discomfort, it establishes the connections with a reachable pledge to mend the situation. Expressing reality also ensures believability, while encouraging the recipient to be even more involved. This prompt should be presented with "I Think" statements. With "I Think" statements, one can be truthful with all parties sans a potential adverse effect. Some examples include "I Think this is the cause of the issue . . . ," or "I Think this is salvageable if . . . ," or "I Think we need to focus on another direction. . . . "

Displaying the reality of the situation is crucial in developing a productive interaction. Thus, the recipient should trust the thought process behind the information given. There will be times in which the facts of the matter will be difficult to express or set a somber undertone. However, as the relationship is managed for positivity and genuineness, with consistent practice, delivering the reality can benefit all stakeholders.

In addition to expressing what you think, there are numerous benefits in respecting the thoughts of the other individuals involved, especially with students. This promotes a practice of thinking before reacting. Reap these benefits by asking "What were your thoughts when . . . " or "I'd like to know what you think . . . " or "Are we thinking the same thing?" Jointly exploring what you both think can potentially lead to new and creative solutions.

## P_otential

This part of the strategy provides the step-by-step approach to find reachable, measureable successes. It also solidifies confidence in the collaborative path to success. If available, the person initiating the conversation should use any similar situations of success to foster confidence in reaching the next level of success. Incorporating "I Believe" statements into the conversation will steadily build the relationship. Similar to sharing the reality, preparing all stakeholders for the range of possibilities can strengthen a relationship, regardless of the outcome. These statements can include, but aren't limited to, "I Believe this is where we'll prosper . . . " or "I Believe we can celebrate this amount of progress when . . . " or "I Believe there will be a breakthrough at this juncture. . . . "

It is important to demonstrate the broad scope of what could potentially take place. Additionally, it may take the initiator of the conversation to help identify potential benchmarks as the relationship grows. In conjunction, expressing a belief in the potential allows for adjustments of these benchmarks so that the goals in the plan have a greater chance of being accomplished. For students, parents, or colleagues, receiving their feedback can be advantageous while asking, "What goals would you like to address?" or "When do you believe we should revisit this?" or "How do you believe we can accomplish this?" or "How are our respective ideas similar?" Due to this, participants in the conversation can exit with a respectable amount of understanding that success doesn't function without collaboration.

## L_everage

The word "leverage" means positional advantage or power to act effectively. Acknowledging the existence of the leverage, without abusing it or overusing it, takes real skill. Impulsively, many would think that leverage lies with the person with the most positional power. In contrast the person, or persons, who have the greatest to gain are the true owners of the leverage. Once identified, the lead communicator should use "realization" statements. These statements can include "I Realized that____, but____" or "Once (name) realizes that they can (behavior), he/she may experience better outcomes" or "It's (name) duty to Realize that this must be completed."

This portion of the strategy can really be recognized when conversing about the growth of the relationship between school personnel and the parent. Usually, acknowledging the leverage during the building of the relationship will ultimately create accountability in the young person involved. For example, Mrs. Franklin spoke to Tammy's mom about Tammy receiving too many class tardy referrals. Instead of Mrs. Franklin abusing her power as an administrator and demanding that Tammy get to class on time or else, she identified the source of the tardy slips as stemming from Tammy loitering in the hall after her lunch period. Now, the responsibility for her behavior is placed with Tammy. Choosing to not loiter gives her the leverage and much to gain: fewer referrals and improved academic achievement.

## E_mpowerment

At this stage of the conversation, normally at the exit point, a classification of roles for success creates empowerment. As a plus, this encourages, motivates, and inspires all stakeholders to make necessary changes to take steps toward agreed upon goals. Using this prompt allows for all participants to benefit in the management of the relationship as it moves forward. Empowerment helps keep everyone at a level of contribution, regardless of the size of the contribution. Empowering statements, or questions, can include, "These additional resources will help you achieve your goals" or "What will be your first steps?" or "How will you move forward from this point?"

So many times people exit conversations measuring the quantity of their personal agenda items being achieved. With empowerment being the last prompt of this strategy, this does not necessarily mean that empowerment has to be introduced last. For the relationship management assurance, this prompt may have to be introduced multiple times. Ultimately, with all parties being empowered, no one can feel slighted as the conversation concludes. As for the young persons involved, empowerment is often enough for them to remain absorbed in the process in order to achieve the desired result. We will now rejoin Mr. Juarez and Ms. Prentice together in the teacher's lounge immediately after school.

*Mr. Juarez was anxious about having a conference with a parent. After numerous sessions with a particular student, Mr. Juarez realized that the student was most likely exhibiting adverse behaviors in order to be purposely sent home on suspension. The student, Justin, admitted that he desired to be at home to care for his mother who was suffering from cancer. Mr. Juarez made his way to the conference room when Ms. Prentice offered her assistance. She was very familiar with the eighth grader from having him in her class in prior years, and she was very aware of his family crisis.*

*Mr. Juarez began sincerely, "Good afternoon, Mrs. Delgado. I'm so glad that you could take the time to make it here. I know your mobility is becoming difficult these days. I hope you don't mind if Ms. Prentice joins us. She knows Justin quite well, and from my understanding, you two have a well-established history." Mrs. Delgado showed obvious signs of receiving chemotherapy, but was very alert. She had been a single mom since Justin was a 4th grader and in Ms. Prentice's class. Everyone had managed to work through that tough transition for Justin's sake, and Ms. Prentice had worked diligently to make sure Justin had a successful year, despite the challenges.*

*Mrs. Delgado confidently replied, "Good afternoon, Mr. Juarez, Ms. Prentice. No, I don't mind at all if she sits in. She was very supportive to me and Justin while he struggled with his dad leaving. Anything that will help Justin." Mr. Juarez began by stating that Justin had received numerous referrals lately, from different teachers. Somewhat unlike him, it had become a concern for his teachers and administration. Mr. Juarez continued with how this particular number of referrals would lead to Justin being sent to In-School Detention and eventually Out-of-School Suspension. Mrs. Delgado quickly rebutted with it not being his fault and that the school should be more lenient under the circumstances.*

*Suddenly, Ms. Prentice interrupted, "Mrs. Delgado, you do know that we all feel the same about Justin. He has great potential, especially since he has come such a long way and continues to progress since 4th grade. We all empathize with your ordeal right now, but the reality is that he cannot continue to behave this way. Now that we know his motivation, we think he can find a better way to deal with the current situation. We believe he needs added confidence and emotional security."*

*Mrs. Delgado looked puzzled, at first. She inquired to know about Justin's motivation to misbehave. After Mr. Juarez's explanation, her puzzled expression transformed into shock. At that point, Ms. Prentice sharply took advantage of the mood and continued with the strategy. "Mrs. Delgado, this is why we believe that it's in his best interest to speak with him immediately so that he can understand this is not the best method to check on you. It makes perfect sense for him to think that we'll suspend him for at least three days so that he can stay with you and care for you. But he'll be damaging his school year, at the worst time of year in the worst grade to do so."*

Mrs. Delgado gathered her thoughts in order to reply, "Well, what do you expect me to do or say to him? I mean, he's wanting to take care of his mother. I think that's pretty mature for a teenager. The least you could do as a school is be more understanding and just let him sit in your office, Mr. Juarez, or something. I definitely don't want him to be suspended but he could be doing worse things to deal with this." "You have a point, ma'am, but like Ms. Prentice mentioned, there's too much at stake for Justin to jeopardize his school career. Now, we believe something else can be implemented in order for him to be successful," replied Mr. Juarez.

Mr. Juarez explained to the distraught mother that he would be willing to accept an email or text from her every afternoon during Justin's elective class. This way, Justin could come to his office and read the message that his mom is doing fine and in good spirits. Ms. Prentice interceded again, "Now, it'll be up to Justin to check in with Mr. Juarez daily. And as much energy you can muster, Mrs. Delgado, please make sure you send an email or text." "I think I can manage that, for the time being at least. There'll be some days when I'm at the hospital for my treatment. But I can still send something from there, I guess," answered Mrs. Delgado with a sigh of relief.

Ms. Prentice added, "I'm sure Justin and all of his teachers will benefit from this routine, and there's still some time for him to get back on track and re-focus on his academics. You know he still can go on to 9th grade with a GPA in the top ten. No doubt you would be very proud of that accomplishment." "Indeed, I would, Ms. Prentice. I apologize if I came off as uncooperative. But I haven't been able to put up much of a fight lately. And when it comes to Justin, I just feel like he's been through enough at a young age that it's hard for me to discipline him."

Both Mr. Juarez and Ms. Prentice reassured Mrs. Delgado that it was not her fault and that she was still doing a great job at parenting. They conversed a bit more about Justin's behavior and ended the conference. Mr. Juarez graciously thanked Ms. Prentice for her assistance with the P.R.P.L.E. strategy and complimented her by saying he could hardly tell that she had only recently begun practicing it. They briefly discussed how each layer was essential, regardless of the order in which each layer was delivered, depending upon the course of the conversation. Mr. Juarez made a personal commitment to practice this delivery for the remainder of the school year.

**Think. Reflect. Connect.**

Think of a time when you had to participate particularly in a challenging conversation with a parent or colleague. Use the questions below to explore how the P.R.P.L.E Sandwich Strategy might have supported your ability to have a mutually beneficial conversation.

- What did you find to be the most difficult part to relay to the other individual?
- What methods have you used to ease the tension about the situation when communicating with the other individual?
- When concluding the conversation, how did all parties exit with clarity and concise steps to improve the situation?
- What follow-up to the initial conversation was used to measure any progress?

One thing to keep in mind is the difference between acknowledging the leverage and announcing the empowerment. Remember that the leverage has some action attached to it. It will require someone to perform a duty, task, or action. As a result of this task being performed, empowerment is the measurable outcome. By having empowerment as an outcome for all parties, each subsequent conversation has the potential to generate more creative and collaboratively developed solutions.

As a reminder, the use of the P.R.P.L.E. Sandwich Strategy techniques do not necessarily have to be in the exact order in which they are written. Each technique can be used in isolation or you might only need to use two to engage in constructive communication. The techniques are:

- Positive—identify a behavior, action, or recall a time when the student demonstrated success.
- Reality—state the actuality of a situation, not an idealistic notion.
- Potential—acknowledge the student's capacity to be or do better. Praise can be valuable with this technique.
- Leverage—acknowledge who has the most to gain.
- Empower—encourage, praise, and elevate the student's thinking to make better decisions or act in a more positive manner.

## FINAL THOUGHTS

As was stated earlier, you may not use all of the techniques together, but it is necessary to layer each prompt in a manner that allows for each participant to have a clear and thorough understanding of the information shared. Therefore, it is helpful to keep pace of the conversation with statement starters, such as "I/We feel, I/We think, I/We believe, and They will realize." A good communicator uses language that invites, supports, and is sensitive to the needs and concerns of those with whom he/she is interacting. By doing this, an effective bridge of communication between all parties is constructed, reinforced, and strengthened.

In the following chapter, Crummell Academy will be revisited. In this new series of scenarios, time has elapsed, and the teachers, administrators, and counselors are facing new and different challenges. As our readers engage with a different set of scenarios, we ask that you view each situation through the lens of, "How does this apply to me?" and "What would I do if faced with a similar situation?" It is our hope that you will be stretched and strengthened in your resolve to apply the strategies of the RMS™ to your lives.

*Section III*

# REFLECTION AND APPLICATION

It is qualitative to know that Crummell Academy, while being a fictitious institution, holds many scenarios that actually occur on a regular basis, in many schools, across this country. These occurrences exceed the amount of incoming teachers who are properly trained or experienced to handle the prelude and aftermath of each occurrence. Due to this situation, those adults who possess genuine talent of relationship management often burn out from the demands of so many interaction deprived young people. Let's hope that the information provided in this book will help you make an effort toward remedying this dire situation.

Section II introduced the reader to several strategies designed to improve the quality of routines and relationships in the classroom. Each strategy was showcased and applied to the teachers introduced in chapter 4, Mr. Locklear, special education teacher, and Ms. Prentice, fourth grade teacher. As a reminder to our readers, the strategies included in the Relationship Management System (RMS)™ are: Monitor 2 Modify (M2M), Relationship Management Pathways (RMPs), D.E.P.T.H. Anchor, and P.R.P.L.E. Sandwich.

*Chapter 9*

# Alexander Crummell Academy—Present Day

Here is a challenging question to consider while reading the account of circumstances and events in Crummell today. When faced with new challenges, how can these teachers move from being effective at implementing the methodologies to being even more effective? We also invite our readers to ask themselves, how does this apply to me? What might I do when faced with similar circumstances? The current realities of the Crummell Academy will be presented in order to provide a context for expanded reflection.

As expected, the demographics at the Crummell Academy continue to change. There is continued growth in the number of African-American students and Latino students and a decrease in the number of Caucasian students. Mr. Warren is in his second year as principal, and Mrs. Franklin continues as assistant principal. Mrs. Franklin and Mr. Warren continue to have significant differences in their approaches; however, they have been united in their attention to implementation of the methodologies designed to improve the quality of relationships and routines within their school. Mr. Juarez and Miss Giovanni are both still working as counselors. Many other teachers have since left the school, but the main characters introduced in chapter 4 remain at Alexander Crummell.

In the following paragraphs, the implementation of Monitor 2 Modify (M2M), Relationship Management Pathways (RMPs), D.E.P.T.H. Anchor, and P.R.P.L.E. Sandwich will be examined within these teachers' classrooms. In subsequent sections of this chapter, the roles of the two administrators, Mrs. Franklin and Mr. Warren, the counselors, Mr. Juarez and Miss Giovanni, as well as the support staff, parents, and even students will be discussed as the reader is invited to dig more deeper through self-reflection and application.

## Ms. Prentice: Monitor 2 Modify (M2M)

*As she plans for her school year, Ms. Prentice has decided to first focus on the Monitor 2 Modify strategy for the initial month or two of school. She remembers that there are three techniques: Firm but Fair, Control without being Controlling, and Reinforce, do not Retreat. While reflecting on her previous classroom experiences, Ms. Prentice is reminded that she has been inconsistent in her implementation of the techniques in the past. She remembers ignoring consistent enforcement of classroom routines and procedures, as she thinks about students challenging her inconsistencies.*

*She has recently learned that a student, John Simpson, who challenged his teachers throughout the preceding year by verbally assaulting other students as well as his previous teacher, will be in her room. Ms. Prentice remembers hearing about John throughout the previous year, because his last year's teacher was heard regularly counting the days before John moved into the next grade. Even before he was assigned to her class, Ms. Prentice is nervous about teaching John.*

*John has been raised by a single mother, who works three jobs to provide for her family, and his attendance has been sporadic. At times, John is absent because his mom depends on him to pick up the slack caused by her commitments at her jobs. He was suspended numerous times during the previous year as a result of his verbally aggressive behaviors.*

*Ms. Prentice is determined to provide consistently utilized routines and strategies to establish and enhance a quality relationship with John. Ms. Prentice wants to plan effectively for her students as the first day of school draws near. As she prepares for the school year, she commits herself to consistent implementation of the three M2M techniques. She reminds herself that the best possible gift she could give John is a positive climate and culture which provides consistent and fairly implemented routines and procedures.*

As she prepares for all students to begin the first day of school, while thinking about John especially, Ms. Prentice works to clearly embed and implement the techniques of the M2M strategy. As a teacher facing the new school year with known challenges, here are some questions for reflection:

- How can Ms. Prentice embed these techniques into her plans for the first weeks of school?
- In what ways can she proactively communicate with her students the three techniques (*Firm, but Fair; Control, without being Controlling;* and *Reinforce, do not Retreat*) from the M2M strategy?
- What might her instruction look like on the first day of school?

*Although Ms. Prentice is committed to implementing these methodologies in an effective way, John comes to class on the first day of school, pushes* another student in the hall as he moves toward the classroom, and yells to Ms. Prentice, "Hey! Why do I have to be in your classroom? I hate this school and I hate you!"

Confronting this challenge on the first day, here are some additional reflective questions to ponder.

- How might Ms. Prentice respond to John in such a way that demonstrates her commitment to build a positive relationship with him as well as establish a clearly understood routine?
- What other actions might Ms. Prentice take on this first day of school?
- What would you do if you were in Ms. Prentice's position?

## Mr. Locklear and Mrs. Brumlett: Relationship Management Pathways

*Mr. Locklear has been assigned a paraprofessional this year, Mrs. Brumlett. Mrs. Brumlett has been in and out of the Crummell Academy since her children were young. She has witnessed the changes in the community over the last several years, and she is vocal about her displeasure at the course of events.*

*Mrs. Brumlett has never been shy about her approach to disciplining students. She raised five children of her own and believes that her way is the correct way. When a student misbehaves, Mrs. Brumlett typically yells loudly and threatens to call that student's parent. Although she is not the primary disciplinarian in the classroom, she frequently tells students that they need to shape up or they will be suspended or expelled indefinitely.*

*Mrs. Brumlett was hired because Mr. Locklear has a couple of new students in his room who need occasional individual assistance with basic skills. Previously, Mrs. Brumlett was at another school working with one student who had a physical disability. The student graduated, and Mrs. Brumlett was transferred to Crummell.*

*As he plans for the first few weeks of school, Mr. Locklear is cognizant of the importance of establishing and maintaining positive relationships with his students, and he is concerned about working as a team with Mrs. Brumlett. Last year, he had worked tirelessly to develop a positive climate with some of the students from his classroom as well as students in some of the other general education classrooms in an effort to promote inclusive practices within the school. His goal was to have some of the general education students mentor some of his special education students. Mr. Locklear's classroom has been segregated, and his students have not been well-received by other faculty or students. He is wondering how he might employ what he knows about RMPs to his classroom.*

*As he thinks about the students in his classroom, he reflects on a few of his students he would like to see take part in more general education classes. Currently, he is thinking about Jermaine, a student who seems to present as a Seeker. Jermaine seeks negative attention from Mr. Locklear by repeatedly asking questions not related to the topic, poking other students in the ribs with his pencil, dropping items on the floor during instruction, and interrupting others when they are talking. Jermaine is a bright student, and he remembers most of what he sees, especially if manipulatives are used and Jermaine has opportunities to move around. Mr. Locklear wants to work with other teachers so that Jermaine starts attending classes outside his special education environment.*

*Complicating this situation is Mrs. Brumlett, whose approach to Jermaine is to yell at him each time he disrupts the environment. Mrs. Brumlett is frequently heard muttering that Jermaine just needs more discipline; it worked for her boys. Mr. Locklear whispers to himself, "Mrs. Brumlett is a Driver, just what I need!"*

Mr. Locklear is faced with finding the most effective approach for Jermaine in order to help him interact effectively in all environments. In addition, Mr. Locklear is challenged by Mrs. Brumlett's comments and her competing with him for control of the classroom. He even ponders suggesting that Mrs. Brumlett participate in the Personality Package webinar. This is the exercise he had completed that had helped him address people, especially young people, with a genuine and positive approach. As you engage the following questions think about your own practices, methods, and techniques.

- In what ways can Mr. Locklear best approach instruction with Jermaine, knowing that Jermaine seeks attention from the adults in the classroom?
- How might Mr. Locklear work with Mrs. Brumlett to improve interactions with her, as he wants to meet Jermaine's needs?
- What steps might Mr. Locklear take in order to help Jermaine be successful in general education classes?
- What other ideas do you have?

*While Mr. Locklear is developing his strategies and plans to work effectively with Mrs. Brumlett, he learns that he will also be receiving another student from another campus. Mr. Locklear is familiar with this student, Tamera, because she is friends with his daughter. Tamera has been reported as avoiding interactions with adults by being unresponsive. Mr. Locklear rubs his brow, muttering to himself, "A Driver as a paraprofessional, a Seeker, and a new Armored student! What am I going to do now?" Mr. Locklear is fully committed to creating a positive culture as he works to integrate his students into the general education classrooms.*

Thinking about Mr. Locklear's challenges, ponder the following questions.

- What changes, if any, need to be made to the plans Mr. Locklear is currently making, in order to accommodate Tamera's unique needs?
- How might Mr. Locklear use what he knows about RMPs to help each individual feel as if s/he were an important part of the classroom environment?
- As he works with a diverse group of students, what do you think would be his most important priorities?
- What strategies would you utilize?

## MS. PRENTICE: D.E.P.T.H. ANCHOR

*One year after being introduced to Relationship Management System (RMS)™, it's October in Ms. Prentice's class. She has experienced some success with her classroom using the M2M strategy, consistently. At times, John speaks out, however, Ms. Prentice pairs her Firm, but Fair technique with much reinforcement. In addition, she is aware that she does not wish to be controlling. She has been seeking opportunities to give John recognition and positive reinforcement for his accomplishments and contributions to the class. She holds students accountable for their behaviors, and she has even instituted a group problem solving routine.*

*Each afternoon, Ms. Prentice meets with a small group of students for the last fifteen minutes of the day to reflect on and identify positive solutions to challenges that have presented themselves. Some topics of discussion have included changing the bathroom procedures and moving the trashcan. Her students seem to have a sense of empowerment, and Ms. Prentice refers to them positively in faculty meetings although some of her colleagues talk about their classes as being made of "little monsters." Ms. Prentice has even worked with her class to craft a class mission statement and a "team" identity. They call themselves the Crummell Champions.*

*What happens next is as much a surprise to Ms. Prentice as to anyone. While walking by the cafeteria on her way to the office, Ms. Prentice sees 5th graders physically harassing a younger student, calling him names because he has a speech impediment. The older students taunt the younger student, laughing at him as he yells at them to "leave him alone!" What is most distressing is that John is in the middle of the fray. Ms. Prentice is disheartened to see John laughing and calling the younger student names as well.*

*Ms. Prentice is faced with a choice. She knows that there are cafeteria supervisors, but she does not see them at a first glance. She also has other options. Ponder the following questions. Think about what you might do, if faced with this situation.*

- What unique challenges are presented with John seeming to be a part of the incident?
- How might the D.E.P.T.H. Anchor work in this situation?
- Considering the components of the D.E.P.T.H. Anchor (Disperse, Emotions, Proximity, Tone, and Help), how might Ms. Prentice accomplish the desired results (Dignity, Even Temperament, Poise, Tenacity, and Health) as she works to diffuse this escalating student interaction, while upholding the foundation of her relationship with John?
- How is this process different from the processes you currently use when faced with similar situations?

## MR. LOCKLEAR: P.R.P.L.E. SANDWICH

*Several weeks have passed since school started, and Mr. Locklear has seen progress in his classroom and how he and Mrs. Brumlett's Personality package allows them to collaborate more productively when they meet on Fridays. He has noticed that Mrs. Brumlett is asking for additional responsibilities, and he is gradually releasing some to her. In addition, Jermaine has been asking about spending time within the general education classroom. Mr. Locklear has identified a teacher, Ms. Saunderson, whom he believes would be able to work effectively with Jermaine in the classroom.*

*However, she is reluctant, since Jermaine's reputation has preceded him. Mr. Locklear has decided that he will use what he knows about the P.R.P.L.E. Sandwich Strategy to advocate for Jermaine's increased participation in the general education class. Working collaboratively with Mrs. Brumlett, Mr. Locklear writes down his thoughts to share in the upcoming meeting. He takes each of the statements and reflects on how he might advocate for Jermaine.*

Mr. Locklear's chief objective is to foster communication and productive collaboration for the purpose of gradually transitioning Jermaine from his segregated setting to Ms. Saunderson's general education classroom. Mr. Locklear knows that Jermaine should in an environment where his talents and gifts might be appreciated and strengthened. Simultaneously, the behavioral challenges he presents must be minimized through the use of the RMS™ strategies.

- If you were in Mr. Locklear's position, how might you work collaboratively with Ms. Saunderson in order to advocate for Jermaine as he transitions from your classroom?
- How would you go about identifying what was most important?
- What other individuals might you work with and in what ways?

Using the P.R.P.L.E. Sandwich for reflection, think about a student for whom your advocacy is needed. Using the P.R.P.L.E Sandwich prompts below, think about how you would craft your conversation to support that student.

- **P**ositive – begin conversation with something positive about student, situation or colleague; include "I Feel" statements: "I feel that _____ has a lot of upside/can really progress/ has shown some growth/ we're getting better at............"
- **R**eality – continue conversation with the reality about the student, situation, or colleague regardless of reverberation; include "I Think" statements: "But I think _____ can benefit from/should try/is finding difficulty/ should continue to/............"
- **P**otential – continue conversation with the potential about the student, situation, or colleague; include "I Believe" statements: "So I (we) believe _____ will be successful/will win as soon as/it's in the best interest if/the best option is.........."
- **L**everage – **if necessary**, begin concluding conversation by signifying where the leverage lies, whether it be with student, entity, colleague, or parent; include "It's Evident" statements: "Since it's evident that _____ has the power to change/control the decision to/has to become motivated/ needs to be motivated............."
- **E**mpowerment – exit conversation with student, or colleague, or parent recognizing the empowerment of current situation/conference taking place; include "This Benefits" statements: "Let's say this benefits _____ as we go forward/when we look ahead/in the long run............."

## MRS. FRANKLIN AND MR. WARREN: RELATIONSHIP MANAGEMENT SYSTEM™

*As Mr. Warren and Mrs. Franklin were completing the first semester, they noticed that behavioral referrals were decreasing and most teachers were using the strategies effectively. While they were discussing their observations, one of the counselors, Mr. Juarez, informed them that a parent had noticed some positive changes in her child. This parent was also interested in some of the strategies for home implementation. Mr. Warren asked Mr. Juarez to work with Miss Giovanni to plan a parent training component. Mr. Juarez agreed to start the conversation with Miss Giovanni immediately.*

The building leaders saw improvements in the student behaviors at Crummell, and they desired to share their techniques with families in an effort to increase effectiveness and expand their collaboration with families. Ponder on the set of questions below.

- How would you go about sharing the RMS™ with families with whom you work?
- What priorities would you stress?
- How can collaboration with families strengthen your relationships with students?
- What steps might you take in building a stronger sense of culture and community in your classroom using the techniques that have been presented?

## Miss Giovanni and Mr. Juarez: Relationship Management System™

*As Miss Giovanni and Mr. Juarez discussed how to implement a supportive parent component, they brought up some of the students who had been impacted by two years of implementation of the RMS™. Some of the positive changes came from a former student of Ms. Prentice using some of the RMS™ language. This student was heard to mutter, "You act like you are the driver of this school, taking everybody on a trip to nowhere!" Although Miss Giovanni knew that the student's word choice was coincidental, it started her thinking about how she and Mr. Juarez might incorporate students into the process of strengthening the RMS™ within the school.*

Mr. Juarez quickly agreed with Miss Giovanni that one of the best things they could do to infuse the RMS™ techniques into the climate and culture of the school was to enlist the collaboration of students. They began to make a list of ideas. First, they both agreed that they would work collaboratively with students to get student leaders to teach new students routines to enhance relationships. They decided to begin with the premise that we are all accountable for climate in classroom.

- What steps do you believe that Miss Giovanni and Mr. Juarez need to take to reinforce that we are all accountable for the classroom climate?
- How would you communicate this message to students?
- How might you teach students ways to incorporate the RMS into their interactions with others?
- How could you help students mentor other students?

### FINAL THOUGHTS

The reader has been asked to stretch his/her thinking by engaging with the faculty and staff at Crummell, while thinking about how the strategies can be applied to new scenarios. Each of the strategies has been revisited using scenarios similar to those that educators regularly face while striving to meet the needs of diverse student populations. The reader has been invited to also think about incorporating families into the process. In addition, opportunities for personal application have been provided.

The authors firmly believe that simply knowing strategies and techniques is not enough. We must also be willing to apply and incorporate these strategies into our day-to-day interactions in the school or classroom, collecting data on their effectiveness and adjusting them, while maintaining the essence of the strategies, to meet our own specific classroom demands.

In the final chapter, the authors will pose new thoughts to assist you in digging deeper to conceptualize how you might engage and encourage colleagues, students and parents using these strategies. The authors will recap highlight the main points of, provide additional resources for professional development and training on the system and other supportive strategies and tools, and will provide some food for thought for administrators and parents.

*Chapter 10*

# Final Thoughts and Next Steps

The authors of this book have a saying, "Everyone thinks they are great with relationships, until they are not!" In many ways, *Success Favors* is based on that quote. At times, we all need to examine the relationships we are developing and the routines and examples that we set in the classroom and in the school for our students. This book is designed to, in part, support educators, school leaders, and other campus personnel, in establishing routines and developing positive relationships that will support the overall learning environment. This book is also designed to be a thinking resource for teachers and others to reflect on how to effectively establish a culture of respect for all. The overarching ideal is to be intentional about every element of relatedness—rapport, respect, responsiveness, and routines.

*Success Favors* offers approaches for working with different, and,j10 sometimes, challenging personalities, and character traits. It is commonly understood that the routines established and the relationships we build with our students can be critical to the perceptions that they have of themselves. Those essentials can also impact the value that students place on education and achievement. Positive interactions, student engagement, empowerment, and achievement are all keys to success. Success, for many students, is a dream deferred or a dream denied. They need adults who will provide a firm structure, who will create an academically safe environment, and people whom they can trust to be authentic and genuinely concerned about their futures.

As the research presented in chapter 2 asserts, classroom management and relationships are reported as the most challenging aspects of teaching for novice as well as veteran teachers. Routines are essential to maintaining order and appropriate control in the classroom. Routines also allow students to recognize and understand the classroom expectations and consequences of misbehavior. Routines provide students with a sense of stability and certainty, as they engage in their learning environments.

Relationships are the other side of the relatedness coin. Students are more likely to work harder, feel safer, and engage more deeply in their work when they have teachers who value their efforts. The relationship that a teacher creates with a student can sometimes be the tipping point for how that student demonstrates persistence, determination, diligence and a host of other social and emotional competencies. Simply put, relationships matter in and out of the classroom, and can be the measuring cup of success for many students.

In chapter 3, the reader was introduced to the Interaction Congruence Theory (ICT). The ICT is comprised of five components that support student achievement, positive interactions, and relatability. These components are: the Personality Package™, Responsiveness, Rapport, Routines, and Respect. These components are particularly helpful to educators, as they develop various approaches to engage students in their academic and social-emotional success.

The Personality Package™ is the foundational part of the ICT because it guides one through an introspective self-analysis. It has been used successfully in various education settings, including K–12, higher education, and alternative education. The process helps adults to identify the characteristics, traits, and dispositions that drive how one interacts with others daily. This process also leads to the development of a personality mantra, which is an affirming tagline for genuine expression from one person to another. Once the Personality Package™ has been developed or identified, the other four components work in concert to distinguish an effective and productive culture and climate for learning.

Responsiveness focuses the teacher's attention on the needs of individual students. This could be the student's academic as well as social and emotional needs. Rapport, in many ways, is characterized by the ways in which students interact with each other and the teacher. Routines are essential to ensuring that the classroom and school functions well. Routines also support efficient use of instructional time and can decrease the opportunity for students to misbehave. Respect is critical to creating a space that reflects the notion that educational achievement is important and that all persons and learning will be valued. Together the intentional culture of learning can be sustained.

Each component of the theory is aligned to strategies that are a part of The Relationship Management System (RMS)™ system introduced in section II. Each strategy, approach, and technique, when used together, can support or enhance a school's current behavior guidance plan. RMS™ can also be implemented as a stand-alone classroom management system that will emphasize a shared belief that reflects pride in self and others. As was mentioned in chapter 5, The RMS™ has been implemented successfully in both large and small, urban, and suburban school districts.

More information on the Personality Package™, workshop topics, strategies, how to assess the effectiveness of RMS™ in your school, and other products developed by Parker Ed. can be found at: www.parkeredanddevelopment.com.

## FINAL THOUGHTS

This book presented some new terminology, perhaps packaged strategies in a new way, or refreshed others' thinking about how to effectively create a classroom environment that will support relatedness. It is the authors' hope that educators will find this book not only useful in their professional lives, but, perhaps, in their personal lives as well. While this book focused primarily on teachers throughout the scenarios and reflections, the authors acknowledge that school leaders, parents, and other campus personnel are essential to effective implementation and constructive support of any routine, procedure, policy, and process. High functioning schools have high functioning and effective stakeholders.

We know that in schools, success favors well-prepared teachers, students, leaders, counselors, and support staff. Therefore, it is the job of all parties to ensure that we are raising the next generation of young people to be well prepared to find their own paths toward success regardless of their backgrounds, histories, or circumstances. Adults, who are not begrudging toward young people as they make mistakes, will find themselves on the receiving end of statements such as, "Hey, I can't believe you were able to get those students to follow that procedure." Just remember, relationships can be seasonal, but proper relationship management will impact how one interacts with others for a lifetime.

# About the Authors

**Todd Scott Parker, MAT, MEd,** is a twenty-year veteran educator, coach, and now, CEO of Parker Education & Development, LLC. He distinguishes himself through his ability to deliver dynamic educational coaching and professional development through his brand of Edu-tainment. He is driven to inspire educators to develop their talents and gifts to be prepared to teach and lead people from diverse backgrounds, cultures, and histories. As an author, poet, and energetic inspirational speaker, Mr. Parker believes that young people deserve adults who are creative, skilled, experienced, and passionate about impacting their lives in a positive and profound way.

Mr. Parker is also the creator and director of Kuu-Bro, a leadership initiative for young men and boys to establish their voice and cultivate their leadership skills. He has also developed a student mentoring program called, A Better Citizen (ABC) currently implemented in alternative education settings. The program has received local and national attention. Through his company, he has developed various strategies to support productive and high-functioning schools. His work has led to making various national presentations and speaking engagements.

## About the Authors

**Candice Dowd Barnes, EdD,** is an associate professor at the University of Central Arkansas in the Department of Elementary, Literacy and Special Education. She is also the Chief Operations Officer for Parker Education & Development, LLC. She strongly believes in the power of authentic learning experiences to teach beyond the walls of the classroom into all aspects of life.

She coauthored *Civility, Compassion and Courage in Schools Today: Strategies for Implementing in K-12 Classrooms.* The 3 Cs promotes teaching civility, compassion and courage in schools, in homes and in the community using the Model of Influence—a framework for that moves from awareness to action. She has presented for both national and international audiences on service-learning, civility in schools, social and emotional learning, coaching, curriculum integration and assessment planning, and disposition development in schools and work settings. She has also authored multiple articles on relationships and various other like-minded topics.

**Patricia Kohler-Evans, EdD,** is a professor at the University of Central Arkansas in the Department of Elementary, Literacy, and Special Education. As a former teacher, she has worked with students with disabilities for over thirty years. She has nineteen years of experience as a special education administrator in the largest district in Arkansas, serving urban students with numerous needs stemming from poverty, disability, and race. While there, she focused on inclusive education and making sure that the needs of all students were met. During her tenure in Little Rock, the district cohosted the state's first conference on inclusive education.

Dr. Kohler's research interests include inclusive education and meeting the needs of all students in various settings. She is the coauthor of *Civility, Compassion and Courage in Schools Today:*

*Strategies for Implementing in K-12 Schools* and *Meaningful Conversations: The Way to Comprehensive and Transformative School Improvement.* The 3 Cs promotes teaching civility, compassion, and courage in schools, homes, and in the community using the Model of Influence—a framework for that moves from creating awareness to action. She has also numerous published articles on co-teaching, the importance of developing positive relationships with students as well as teachers. She serves as an executive coach for the Little Rock School District.

www.ingramcontent.com/pod-product-compliance
Lightning Source LLC
Chambersburg PA
CBHW021847220426
43663CB00005B/432